Death Metal

A 33⅓ SERIES

Forthcoming in *Genre: A 33 1/3 Series*

Death Metal

T Coles

BLOOMSBURY ACADEMIC
NEW YORK • LONDON • OXFORD • NEW DELHI • SYDNEY

BLOOMSBURY ACADEMIC
Bloomsbury Publishing Inc
1385 Broadway, New York, NY 10018, USA
50 Bedford Square, London, WC1B 3DP, UK
29 Earlsfort Terrace, Dublin 2, Ireland

BLOOMSBURY, BLOOMSBURY ACADEMIC and the Diana logo are
trademarks of Bloomsbury Publishing Plc

First published in the United States of America 2023

Library of Congress Cataloging-in-Publication Data
Names: Coles, T (Music journalist), author.
Title: Death metal/T Coles.
Description: [1st.] | New York: Bloomsbury Academic, 2021. | Series:
Genre: a 33 1/3 series | Includes bibliographical references. |
Summary: "Guides readers through an overview of death metal, broken
down to explore its foundations, tropes and myriad microgenres and
presented for an outsider with a morbid curiosity but little
experience"– Provided by publisher.
Identifiers: LCCN 2022008924 (print) | LCCN 2022008925 (ebook) |
ISBN 9781501381010 (paperback) | ISBN 9781501381027 (epub) |
ISBN 9781501381034 (pdf) | ISBN 9781501381041
Subjects: LCSH: Death metal (Music)–History and criticism.
Classification: LCC ML3534.C639 2021 (print) |
LCC ML3534 (ebook) | DDC 781.66–dc23
LC record available at https://lccn.loc.gov/2022008924
LC ebook record available at https://lccn.loc.gov/2022008925

ISBN: PB: 978-1-5013-8101-0
          ePDF: 978-1-5013-8103-4
          eBook: 978-1-5013-8102-7

Series: Genre: A 33 1/3 Series

Typeset by Integra Software Services Pvt. Ltd.
Printed and bound in Great Britain

Contents

Acknowledgements

Enormous thanks to my wonderful editor Ryan Pinkard for his tireless work and rapid absorption of extreme metal facts and mythology, and to Chris French, my go-to death metal consultant who provided much-needed advice and perspective. The hardest parts of this were made joyful because of your efforts.

Huge love to Amy Martin, Leah Babb-Rosenfeld, Rachel Moore and the team at Bloomsbury who helped bring this project to fruition. You were truly lovely to work with and helped de-mystify the process of writing and releasing a book.

The mightiest of hails to everyone who contributed interviews, and to my dear friends and collaborators: Ross Dickinson, Sam Ferrins, Stewart Ross, Perrie Codling, Frankie Brown, Freya Jeffries and the Exeter writing group, Aimée and Alex Wyld, Faye Thomas, Elle Romaine, Andy Douglas, Tom Lawton, Billy Holt, Catriona Morrison, Arianna Albayati, Sam Bromage, Laura Abbott, Seb Male, Jojo Cranwell, Nicolete Burbach, Emma Grisdale, Ross Brownell (particularly for football and professional wrestling facts), Charlotte Justice and everyone at OHT, Kez Whelan, Darren Sadler, Bobby Barry, Chris Grenville, Eden Kupermintz, Bethany Aston, and James, George and Tom Kenchington: thank you for your support at every stage of this book. You have aided the cause of death metal and will be rewarded in Valhalla.

Deep love and gratitude to my band members Charlie Dowzell, Tim Kazer and Kynan Scott, who provided me with much-needed music theory clarification, put up with me disappearing for weeks, and absorbed unsolicited Bolt Thrower trivia. Regular touring will now commence.

Love and respect go to the good PR folk who helped make this happen: Andy Turner, Joe Naan, Claire Harris, Becky Laverty, Silke Yli-Sirniö and Adam Sagir. You were all great and don't get thanked enough for the work you do, so here is a section just for you.

A cheery thanks to the following, who sent me their favourite bands and kicked off some interesting discussions: Mike Cook, Tom Moss, Max James, Rodney Fuchs, Phil Walker, Jozef Allen, April Bishop, Jon Rhodes, Tom Williams, James Millis, Adam Wilde, Steffan Benham, Eli Pearson, Rhys Stevenson, Ricky Wilmot, Curtis Edwards, Chris Gerlgern, James King, Steve Roberts, Luke Oram, Steve Evans, Ross Staffin, Dan Dolby, David Stallard, Mark Sanders, Jimbob Isaac, Rod Reinhardt, Neil Criddle, Innes Maxwell, Tom Varden, Tony & Josh Giles, Carl Flynn, George Parr, Chainy Rabbit, Phil Oberheinrich, Adam Pegg, Dave Hamilton-Smith, Tom Abbey, Abi Ghoulson, Will Robinson, Jean-Francois Garnero, Franklyn Andrews, Simon Clark, Danny Robertson, John Tron Davidson, Wouter Hommel, Wayne Boucher, Joel Oxley and Matt Ainsworth.

Particular thanks to Glenn Charman, who got us all hooked on death metal way back. This book exists because of your influence.

To my parents, Simon and Sarah: thank you for everything, especially teaching me to read, which was useful in the writing and editing stage. To my siblings Ruby, Zoe and Megan: thank you for your support whilst I was writing this and for growing up with the early research. I hope this book is easier to digest than the music.

Finally, thanks to Jason Bidmead, the music technician who played me Cannibal Corpse as a joke when I was thirteen. I am afraid things have gotten wildly out of hand.

1   You suffer, but why?

In 2017, Ed Miliband, once a serious contender for the UK's prime minister, hosted an afternoon show on BBC Radio 2.[1] Filling in for regular personality Jeremy Vine, his star guest was Napalm Death vocalist Barney Greenway. To the delight of everyone else, Miliband requested that he teach him to sing the classic 'You Suffer', the world's shortest song, at 1.316 seconds. Greenway, to his credit, gave it a go.

This went predictably. Within hours, tech-savvy metal heads had overlaid Miliband's reedy attempt onto the original audio[2], and were gleefully tweeting clips of it.

While on air, Greenway was presented with a selection of listeners calling in. One of them simply told him his music was unlistenable, which left him unfazed. Being the clued-in sort, he knew what he was in for; the producers had called the segment 'Why Does Anyone Like Death Metal?' after all.

And then, a curious thing happened. People called in with real stories of devotion that seemed to go cheerfully against the grain. Far from being treated as a novelty, Greenway was regarded with a respect that ranged from begrudging to wholly sincere. Shortly afterwards, reports surfaced that Napalm Death's streams had risen by 228 per cent,[3] buoyed no doubt by the band's rapturous (and overdue) appearance at Glastonbury Festival. It's worth noting that Miliband is back on the frontlines of UK politics at time of writing, his career not even slightly dented for his foray into the noisier end of extreme metal.

This is an excellent point of entry for death metal. What other form of music compels the good folk of England to abandon their stations in the afternoon to complain about its very existence? Or has left such a mark on the fabric of alternative culture that it was deemed suitable for discussion by a former leader of Her Majesty's Opposition?

Death metal inspires stories like this. The music is ugly and lumpen, jagged, foreboding and inaccessible, even by the adolescent standard of broader metal genres. Lyrically, themes range from unbelievably vile depictions of gore and torture, bizarre and unpleasant takes on mysticism, vast futuristic landscapes, and dense and complex hammer blows of sociopolitical theory. The history reads like a very loud underdog story, undulating between surprising success, deeply entrenched battles from within, financial hardships, and a never-ending push against technical possibility and the boundaries of taste.

And yet, undeniably, death metal is enduring and vital, a scrappy genre that brings as much joy to its followers in the 2020s as it did at its inception nearly forty years ago.

The Ed Miliband episode is a rare instance where death metal was exposed to unfiltered reactions from an otherwise unassuming general public. But death metal is a strange and arcane beast, even to those who know and love it. Before we ask *why* anyone likes it, we can ask: *What is death metal? How is it made? And why would anyone make it?*

What is death metal?

Barney Greenway was one of the first people I spoke to for this project, and he was very careful to note that he doesn't consider Napalm Death to be a death metal band in the strictest sense. Though their modern sound is more varied and experimental, death metal has developed far beyond the movement they helped kickstart in the early 1980s. What they've kept is their ferocity, their harsh vocal style and their will to confront people with severe topics like human rights and the perils of neoliberal capitalism. To make things more complicated, *You Suffer* is generally considered to be grouped under the 'grindcore' category – more on that later.

In any case, not all death metal sounds like this, or discusses these topics. *So what is it?*

'It was a natural progression really, from heavy metal to what became known as thrash metal,' says Carcass guitarist Bill Steer, who, as a one-time member of Napalm Death, was there for the genre's earliest rumblings. 'Then, very rapidly, it was an offshoot which people called death metal.'

Death metal is part of the umbrella of 'extreme metal', a larger category of subgenres that push the standard metal sound in a more intense, abrasive direction. To achieve this, one can imagine the sound of earlier metal bands – bombastic stalwarts from the New Wave of British Heavy Metal (NWOBHM) like Judas Priest or Iron Maiden, or the pacier, frantic thrash of Metallica or Anthrax – but driven to extremes of volume and speed.

Death metal's core features warp and weave between releases, disciplines and bands, but largely they can be boiled down to (1) guttural 'death growl' vocals, (2) distorted and de-tuned bass and guitars and (3) ribcage-shattering double kick drums. These kinetic methods bulldoze the listener. Their combined might is cacophonous and overwhelming. It is from this base that death metal's legacy is built, with subsequent movements adding or subtracting layers to improve on the formula.

While death metal sounds indescribably foul to the casual listener, it is a wildly inventive domain, and musicians dedicate their entire lives to creating the perfect sound within its boundaries.

Consider the blast beat, where the drums play a lightning-fast rhythm, largely devoid of groove, with the express purpose of pummelling the listener into oblivion. To capture the feeling of being obliterated, it is useful to describe the classic version in technical terms. In traditional rock beats – say in AC/DC's track *Back in Black* – the drummer might hit the snare once every four beats. In a typical blast beat, the bar is separated into sixteenths, with the drummer hitting the snare eight times, alternated between hits of the bass drum and cymbal. This is played at outlandish speeds, to the absolute limits of human ability. There are enough variations on this beat to fill any number of 33 1/3 books, but the uniting aim is to drive the rhythm forward by any means necessary. Of course, bands like Agoraphobic Nosebleed have taken this further by bringing in drum machines to play louder, longer and faster, eliminating the weaknesses of the flesh.

'I like the physicality,' opines Ryan Sheperson, drummer of sci-fi themed newcomers Cryptic Shift. 'It's always challenging. When I'm pushing myself more it's kinda great to be aware of when I can nail a track. It feels like an accomplishment to me because I'm battling against the limitations.'

Elsewhere, the guitars and basses are often tuned as low as possible, playing dazzling repeated riff patterns or blunt strikes. Death metal guitars are often augmented by effects pedals, a notable example being the Boss HM-2, a grimy distortion pedal that makes the guitar sound like a chainsaw cutting through anthills.

'Across metal, in all senses, you're nothing without the riffs,' confirms Steer. 'Really that's the main currency.'

Death growl

Most central to death metal's identity are the famously low, raw vocals. Described as the death growl, and often referred to in jest as 'cookie monster' vocals, this is a technique by which the vocalist sings from the depths of their diaphragm, contorting their throat to create a guttural effect that resembles the death throes of a wounded animal. It is a dramatic and deeply unpleasant sound that leaves the lyrics butchered and unintelligible. Whilst other aspects are endlessly mutable, with some death metal sounding slow and ponderous, or clean and bright, it's difficult to make identifiable death metal without this technique.

'People are like, *how did death metal become death metal?*' says Metal Blade Records founder and CEO Brian Slagel. 'Well, you can only go so heavy with singing vocals, and the only way to make it heavier is to have the vocals be as heavy as they could be.'

'I look at death metal vocals as almost a percussive instrument,' explains Gatecreeper vocalist Chase Mason. 'You're not singing, so you've got to let the guitars take over the melodic parts in the music and then the vocals are more a percussive instrument where the cadence can still make it catchy.'

How does the death growl have such an impact? I sought out the music scholar Paul Hegarty to explain. In his book *Noise/Music: A History*, he outlines the idea of 'noise' as a cultural and political statement against notions of taste, an evolving assault on the senses that adapts with ever-changing boundaries, and a framework that links the rebellious intentions of punk, industrial and electronic noise artists. I saw parallels with the evolving nature of death metal. Part of its story is that it challenges musicians to play faster, harder and louder, and disgusts its own audience with graphic displays of violence, not to mention repulsing responsible pearl-clutching types who loathe it with a religious fervour.

'The noise bit for me is what you're doing for the expectation of the voice,' Hegarty explains about the death growl. 'What's it doing to the expectation of communication? What happens to a word when it's death growled at high speed?'

When I first heard a death growl, I was shocked and amused. It was funny that someone would take a heavy metal song and use the vocals in this way, especially when I'd heard Iron Maiden classics where the epic vocals soared into the higher registers. That style is great for describing the fantastical tales of powerslaves or ancient mariners, but not so effective for a more visceral description of death.

Hegarty highlights the idea that, through the death growl, communication of words is mangled, subverting expectations and ideas of melody that are common throughout pop music and even other extreme styles of heavy metal. Ed Miliband learned this directly; 'You Suffer' is less a song and more a howl into the void. Hearing an inexperienced practitioner such as Miliband might even have been a 'noisy' or transgressive experience to hardened death metal fans.

Despite this, death metal generally isn't formless. It's a far cry from records like Lou Reed's *Metal Machine Music* or Merzbow's *Pulse Demon.* Many of the discussions I had while researching this book devolved into listing death metal songs that had some catchy quality – classics like Obituary's 'Chopped in Half', Cannibal Corpse's 'Hammer Smashed Face' and At the Gates's 'Slaughter of the Soul'. Whilst there are plenty of moments where death metal wrote something that wasn't remotely structured – 'You Suffer' being the ideal example – there are more instances of bands having success with tracks that did have a strict architecture lurking under the surface.

Gatecreeper's Chase Mason made a similar point when he told me,

> Something that I think sets us apart is writing songs with traditional death metal elements but in a standard pop song structure, like verse-chorus-verse-chorus. If you listen to [classic death metal] records like [Carcass's] *Heartwork* or [Deicide's] *Once Upon the Cross*, they have choruses. They might not have the soaring melodic vocals but they have hooks. That's the classic death metal that I really relate to.

How is it made?

Producer Colin Marston has been recording and playing death metal since the early 2000s, working with bands like Artificial Brain and Defeated Sanity alongside his own projects – such as the baffling Behold the Arctopus – and running his studio, Thousand Caves. When we spoke, I asked him about the unique challenges that a death metal producer faces:

'Mixing is fundamentally relativity,' he says. 'Something is only loud if there's something quieter than it. You're dealing with a kind of music where every instrument has to seem like it's the loudest in the mix. Death metal is the hardest music to mix because everything has to sound like it's the loudest.'

Marston speaks for the struggles of many engineers who take on the mantle of trying to commit death metal to tape, maintaining structure and coherency whilst balancing the rawness of the music and using the production to convey a gruesome or discombobulating message.

'A large percentage of metal bands want the drums to sound like a jackhammer or a piece of industrial machinery,'

Marston continues. 'With the guitar I feel like it's just a question of the same stuff you have in rock and blues, but just pushed further: more distortion, more extreme EQ-ing to create this mean, ridiculous, over the top, dynamic-less, beating-you-over-the-head-with-a-cinderblock kind of sound.'

Giving voice and shape to these recordings is to try to capture instruments at war with themselves and their limitations, and the story of death metal production unfolds with a lot of people who were simply mystified by teenagers attempting to capture something so ghastly.

'That's the thing that's beautiful about metal,' adds Marston. 'You have all these instruments that are trying to do this thing that they can't do, but we're making them do it anyway, damn it.'

So once a record is made, who would release such a thing into the world? Death metal may be an underground and occasionally anti-capitalist world, but it can't escape the commodification of music. Although the economic history of death metal is a turbulent one, the industry now has several niche but formidable labels – including Century Media, Twenty Buck Spin, Napalm Records and Nuclear Blast – that work to put out highly produced death metal records, generally alongside other extreme music. To the untrained ear this prompts questions such as: *How do people make commercial value judgments?*

I posed this to Brian Slagel, who heads one of the leading death metal labels, Metal Blade Records. Now boasting a roster that includes Cattle Decapitation, The Black Dahlia Murder and Job for a Cowboy, they're also responsible for launching the career of death metal titans Cannibal Corpse with the release of their first record, 1990's *Eaten Back to Life*.

'A lot of people, especially people who aren't huge fans of death metal, will say, "Oh it all sounds the same." Well, not really,' says Slagel. 'What people fail to realise is that vocally there are certain melodies – there's a lot of melody that exists in those vocals and the music, and the melody has to be there for me to like it.'

Like most genres, labels provide funds for recordings, PR, tour support and a badge of legitimacy for bands. Functionally there are no major differences in how they work as opposed to other rock or pop labels, albeit with slightly less financial clout behind them. This wasn't always the case, as this story will tell, but it gives insight into how things work behind the scenes, and how death metal tastemakers make important decisions.

Part of having a strong underground means that labels need to pay particular attention to the underground, maintaining links to smaller labels and independent artists that promote promising acts from the grassroots.

'In the last 2 to 3 years we're seeing the labels signing some really interesting new bands that are really young,' Slagel explains. 'I think we're gonna see a new breed of these bands that are going to start doing really well.'

Who makes it?

What does a death metal fan look like? Your prototypical specimen might be sporting long hair and a beard, tattered blue jeans or combat shorts, and a band T-shirt proudly displaying their friends and heroes. Chosen for practicality and an aversion to flamboyant pageantry, these cheap garments are easy to wear on stage or in a crowd, easy to clean and easily obtainable. They're also lurid, featuring graphic scenes from album artwork or disgusting and sometimes indecipherable logos. You'll also notice a notable lack of stage makeup or elaborate hairstyles, a stark contrast to the hair metal of the previous generation.

While fashion changes over time, sometimes facing a direct challenge from people questioning the norm, this style continues through the ages. Death metal fans will maintain these styles well into middle and old age, and it's not unusual to see teenagers and fans in their fifties dressed in similar ways.

Disciples discover death metal in all sorts of places. At one time it was through tape trading, record stores and zines; today through Spotify playlists, Bandcamp recommendations and social media. Then and now, word of mouth is king. There is still a thrill in finding something that feels forbidden, even if it is readily available. Given the variety of bands, it attracts all sorts: geekier folk who like to dig into the mythology of Viking metal pioneers Amon Amarth, literary types who find lots to pore over in bands like Sweden's prog titans Opeth, and revellers who find plenty of hard bangers in sillier acts like Party Cannon.

Death metal is also played all over the world. *So how did it spread from early locations like England and America to current-day strongholds like Scandinavia, Australia and Japan?*

'You had this very decentralised underground that sometimes took hold in particular locations,' says sociologist and author of *Extreme Metal: Music and Culture on the Edge*, Keith Kahn-Harris. 'That model, where it was spreading out from a point of origin, that's sometimes true but it often wasn't; often it was people largely working on their own.'

Connected and disseminated by the early tape-trading scene, which has since been largely replaced by the internet, these undercurrents of interest go some way to explain where interest in this music came from, and how it could spring up so quickly. Thinking in such a way helps to demystify early questions over the start of the genre, and how ideas could develop simultaneously in Tampa, Florida and Birmingham, England.

So within this global underground phenomenon, what kind of person actually makes death metal?

'I think if you're talking about that today I think it's almost impossible to give a general answer,' Kahn-Harris continues.

> Metal culture has become so global and so diverse and so complicated that it's quite difficult to make general statements. With death metal you have to distinguish the decentralised global underground from which it emerged, where it's very difficult to make statements about who these people actually were, from localised scenes that did have a particular character. Tampa is of course the most obvious example – and it does seem to have a blue collar-ish white male element – but there's always exceptions to that.

Early, albeit rare, exceptions to the white, blue collar male death metal archetype include people like Terrance Hobbs, the Black guitarist from Suffocation or Jo Bench from Bolt Thrower, one of the few female death metal musicians from the 1980s. Today the scene has diversified considerably, and it's not unusual to see women of colour, such as Tatiana Shmailyuk from Jinjer, or queer musicians such as Cynic's Paul Masvidal. And whilst the early scene was made of young people in their teens and early twenties, today's death metal family includes people of all ages, all the way to the Grindmother, a death growler born in 1948. Given the subject material and the love that people so clearly have for performing it, it's unsurprising how we ended up with a wider than average demographic of practitioners. Death comes for everyone, after all.

Politics

'Death metal sees politics as a bit pathetic,' says David Burke, a PhD student studying the links between extreme metal and existentialism. 'You can imagine the words of a death metal fan: "I care not for social constructs. I am a free individual. I am a free thinker. Your pathetic politics mean nothing to me."'

While death metal is deeply concerned with the big questions in life – particularly those surrounding death – its attitude towards politics is much less clear cut than its close cousin, thrash metal, which was imprinted with the attitudes of hardcore punk. This sometimes carried over to bands like Napalm Death and Carcass, who are strident defenders of social causes such as animal rights and climate justice. But for the majority of bands, engaging with politics is an option that is often rejected.

'The problems of the human race are so overwhelming that to assess them is merely to describe their horror,' Burke continues. 'That kind of universalised social critique means that for death metal, doing politics seems a little farcical.'

Death metal is dealing with life's one certainty, so it's not surprising why the ever-shifting game of politics looks a little trivial. Of course, over several decades the culture at large has changed, and the attitudes and imagery expressed by some death metal bands are subject to a more robust challenge, especially in regards to the depiction of women in lyrics and artwork, as well as race, gender, sexuality and representation in the scene.

'People joke about how nerdy and virginal metal is, and if there's one *really* virginal bit of metal, it's death metal,' says Tom Dare, former *Terrorizer* editor and host of the podcast *Hell Bent for Metal*, which explores extreme metal from an LGBT+

perspective. 'Generally, death metal doesn't like thinking about sex very much, aside from a few more socially aware bands. Cattle Decapitation has a song called "Forced Gender Reassignment," so they're obviously a little more aware of issues like that.'

'In terms of my work talking about race and extreme music I find [death metal] to be conservative,' says Laina Dawes, author of the 2012 book *What Are You Doing Here?*, an exploration of the intersection between race and gender in extreme metal.

Despite its aversion to politics, the story of death metal often directly overlaps it. And as time has gone on, its stance has continued to evolve.

'It's common for people to say "No politics in my death metal,"' Burke notes, 'though that has to be caveated – things are very different to 10 years ago.'

Gallows humour

For comedians, death metal is a goldmine. Comics such as Stewart Lee, growing up in the UK's grim midlands, recall his youth orienteering with former Napalm Death frontman Nik Napalm. Others theme their whole routines around the genre, with Andrew O'Neill singing 'Hammer Smashed Face' to demonstrate the awesome power of metal to an unsuspecting crowd, or Steve Hughes describing the futility of people breaking into his house looking for money, only to find he has already spent it on 300 death metal CDs.

In shows like *Friends*, groups like Carcass are referenced as an unlikely musical choice for the happy-go-lucky character, Phoebe Buffay. Members of Carcass would later appear as Smeg and the Heads, old bandmates of Dave Lister, the slacker lead of science fiction sitcom *Red Dwarf*. Playing tunelessly, they highlight the folly of his earlier musical ambitions – a little treat for eagle-eyed fans.

A more extreme example is the Adult Swim cartoon *Metalocalypse*, which depicts death metal act Dethklok living a life of wild excess, having made enough money to live in a gigantic castle ('Mordhaus') and travel by the 'Dethkopter', a heavily armed private aircraft. Their vast wealth is maintained through grand performances to legions of devotees and endorsements such as jingles for coffee adverts, and their misadventures frequently result in dramatic injuries and death.

'*Metalocalypse* is a show with a perverse logic,' David Burke advises. 'How could a death metal band be the 7th biggest economy? How could that make sense?'

How indeed? Death metal is inherently a little silly, and often inspires outsiders to laugh awkwardly. Some bands embrace this, like Cannabis Corpse, who trade on weed-themed puns, Stovokor, the Klingon-themed group from Portland, Oregon who perform in traditional battle garb or Nekrogoblikon, goblin devotees who imagine the fate of a creature doomed to a mundane office existence in the video for 'No-one Survives'.

Humour is part of the comprehension of dying. The condemned man could laugh at their bitter fate as the hangman leads him to the gallows, and people suffering together could laugh at their situation, transforming their misery into shared joy. The tension between working to comprehend a deeply serious subject and laughing at the ridiculous results is something at makes the creation of death metal compelling. It's also something that makes it fun for long-time listeners, an unresolved battle between taking something deathly seriously and weeping with laughter. For musicians, humour is one of the many paths they can take on their quest to understand death. For death metal newcomers, laughter is a completely valid response.

Why make it?

'The really simple answer is the most obvious I could give you,' says David Burke, 'which is death'.

When we talk on a drizzly May evening, hooking our laptops up in our spare rooms and making the best of our shoddy internet connections. Given that it is dark out, and we are living through a rough time in the Covid-19 pandemic, we are both in the mood to discuss the fear of death.

'People make death metal for several reasons, which are all connected to death,' he elaborates.

> The first one is the fascination with things that you can't symbolise – what in [French psychoanalyst Jacques] Lacan's work is called 'the Real'. The Real is everything outside of symbolisation. Everyone in metal has a really deep fascination with this realm of the inexplicable and the reason for that fascination emerges effectively from the existential crisis posed by postmodernity. The best way that I've been able to summarise this is that metal challenges the crisis of meaning by asserting the final certainty of death.

In other words, death comes for us all. Making death metal confronts and celebrates this inevitability, the one guaranteed shared experience for everyone on the planet.

As a result, we have a lot of art that concerns death: from the gristly trope of the 'memento mori', to John Everett Millais's painting 'Ophelia', to Richard Wagner's musical drama

'Siegfried's Funeral March'. But while these pieces are dignified and graceful, death is often the opposite.

Burke goes on, 'The second reason is that death metal is all about the radical transformation of the human body, and the most obvious radical transformation of the body you can get is death. It deals with the anxiety of death by envisioning every possible death. It has a song for every kind of dying – it's like a methodical cataloguing of death.'

This is certainly true from a deep dive into the genre, from the myriad forms of torture in Cannibal Corpse and Autopsy, themes of old age and illness in Death, psychological torment in Napalm Death, and arcane deities and rituals in Morbid Angel. Later examples can be a little more nuanced in their exploration of death, as the genre works through the long list of gristly fates. The threat from extraterrestrial beings, for example, is given bizarre life and detail in Blood Incantation's 2019 album, *Hidden History of the Human Race*. It is no surprise that people would turn to an aggressive style of music to confront these formidable feelings and subjects. Abstract or unlikely though these fates may be, they all end in the same way: death.

During my interview with Burke, I tried to think back to when I first heard this sort of music. I was thirteen when a substitute music teacher played my class Cannibal Corpse as a joke. This will probably mark me out as a poser, but I didn't really think it was serious, and was astonished that so much similar music existed. It certainly dealt with death more directly than some of the loud and exciting music I'd been exposed to – mostly mid-2000s emo or punk music that concerned itself with emotional or systemic issues. To be confronted with these humanity-stripping moments at such volume, with a solid bass thud that encourages listeners to slam against one another like a writhing mass of insects was an overwhelming experience, even if my attraction to it felt impossible to understand at the time.

What drew me to it was the volume; it consumed me while directly challenging my definition of what music was. I wasn't especially musical, but some of my closest friends were training to be guitarists and singers, and they were revolted by Behemoth and Entombed. I was torn. I couldn't explain to them why I was drawn to Deicide more than blink-182, and I wasn't sure how seriously I should take it, or whether some of the things they were describing – murder, rape and mutilation – even ought to be committed to music. I was also at odds as to how the death growl could communicate anything when the method of sharing concepts and information was so badly corrupted.

'This is one of the central tensions in metal, between pointing at nothingness – pointing out that you are going to be ripped to shreds by a combine harvester – and doing this through the most ludicrous riffing,' Burke muses. 'The important thing for me is that this is a paradox that does not resolve. Contradiction, paradox, and ambiguity are core to the metal experience – to being metal, to understanding metal, to listening to metal – it all relies on contradictions and paradoxes that get held in tension, that don't resolve properly.'

Burke points out the clash between the busyness of a ridiculous death metal riff or barked grunt, and the fact that bands are singing about the empty void of death. There is power in confronting nothingness by making the loudest noise possible, and an argument that playing or singing as hard as you can is a good way to spite death, raging against the dying of the light.

Death metal is not the only music that grapples with death. When Nick Cave and Kylie Minogue sing about a gruesome assault in 'Where the Wild Roses Grow', they contemplate the fragility of beauty and the ugliness of murder. On 'Life's a Bitch', Nas copes with the imminence of death and potential meaninglessness of life from the perspective of an inner city drug dealer. And on 'Sidewalk Safari', Chairlift daydream about committing a murder, settling on vehicular homicide. These musicians lay it out straight for us, and we can hear what they're singing; it's up to us to think about death, but there are fewer barriers. To be alone with your thoughts and a Cannibal Corpse record requires a higher degree of patience, checking back over the lyric book to work out what they're saying while digesting the sonic bombardment.

In this sense, death metal is in tension with itself, and this shapes a lot of its internal attitudes, towards its audience and its detractors. It also helps humanize what can be an unapproachable style, as the practitioners are dealing with their own fear of the unknown, which comes out as an anxious, jagged mess. When I have played death metal, I've certainly felt like the ideas in the lyrics could be better explained when written down or spoken in a calm, collected manner. But over decades the death growl has become a cultural signifier of the content of death, and the thing that grips an audience and holds their attention.

Passion

The tension between absolute nothing and absolute everything gives death metal a lot of space to explore emotions. With the exception of some avant-garde movements like harsh noise wall or danger music, there are few sounds made by humans that sound as wilfully unpleasant, and certainly none that have been as popular. Death metal is by nature confrontational, often seeking to repulse, unsettle and perturb. This drive to challenge the listener beyond even strained boundaries of conventional taste is the thread that unites bands as disparate as Venom Prison, Gorguts, Morbid Angel and Insect Warfare. But the passion to confront or challenge an audience is not always a negative one.

'Whether it's the lyrics or just the feel, it makes you feel powerful,' Chase Mason comments. '[An album] like *Wolverine Blues* by Entombed makes me feel like I could crush a building with my bare hands.'

These intense emotions unite a great many practitioners across a great gulf of styles.

'Thrash and hardcore were about aggression and brutality. Death metal was a more emotional music style played on different scales – more depressive, more melancholic,' says Tomas Lindberg, vocalist of At the Gates, frontrunners of Scandinavia's 1990s scene. 'It should make you feel uneasy. It should not be comforting.'

'I had in my head an idea that there must be something like death metal before I'd ever heard it,' agrees Anaal Nathrakh and Benediction vocalist Dave Hunt. 'I was seeking out something with that transgressive edge that could act as catharsis for what was going on in my head. It seems a little bit ridiculous to think of music as being dangerous, but back in the day it felt like that.'

It's no surprise that death metal evokes such a range of emotions. These are all valid ways to feel about death, and the passion that marks the genre out is something that's kept a fanbase engaged for decades.

Why write a book about it?

When we consider all these questions, it gives us a sense of death metal's character. With the benefit of many of the bands already mentioned here, we begin to see how death metal is made out of lots of different personality traits. It can be dour, funny, wildly experimental or staunchly traditional. And if these clash or combine, it's because it's made by humans, who are by nature messy.

If you are a newcomer, this book will guide through the permeations of a strange movement, from bands being shunned by recording studios to the modern age where Pitchfork can give Blood Incantation's *Hidden History of the Human Race* an 8.3,[4] beating, at various points, mainstream releases such as U2's *How to Dismantle an Atomic Bomb* (6.9)[5] or Coldplay's *Rush of Blood to the Head* (5.1).[6] It's easy to look at death metal as something ugly and worthy of contempt, but for the morbidly curious, the earnest respect it clearly commands and its odd longevity mark it as worthy for attention.

This brief history gives us insight into how teenagers waking up in the mid-1980s were compelled to make a tremendous racket with this specific aesthetic. There has been no end to groups or movements that aimed to shock; various goth, punk and experimental artists have worked to create a similar effect. But death metal's legacy, whilst certainly not unchanged, has remained largely consistent through its lifespan.

This book is 40,000 words long. *Encyclopaedia Metallum*, a colossal internet database of groups and releases, lists over 50,000 death metal bands. Tempting though it was to list every band Genesis-style, there simply isn't space (and in any case they omitted Gut Rot, the terrible band I formed as a teenager for two afternoons in 2010). Personal disappointments aside, the death metal universe is staggeringly vast and rapidly expanding. Whilst this book cannot cover the history in exhaustive detail – and for the die-hards, will surely omit many worthy bands – it covers the salient points to illustrate how a movement that almost exclusively discusses death could have such staying power.

Detail is paramount to a death metal audience, who have spent years building their knowledge and understanding of the genre. There are plenty of excellent, easily obtainable further resources, like Albert Mudrian's *Choosing Death* and Daniel Ekroth's *Swedish Death Metal*, and documentaries such as Sam Dunn's 'Extreme Metal' episode of his *Metal Evolution* series which all go into microscopic detail as to how this all came about.

This book tells a broader story of death metal, with the intention of uncovering how we go to the point where its most famous practitioners are invited on daytime radio shows. Whilst it's tempting to think about it in terms of movements, it is a human history, full of wild ideas, crushing failures and unlikely successes that people paid dearly for. In these pages, the history is traced from the genre's early roots through various movements into the current day, as we trudge into the 2020s.

So why death metal? The surprising answer might be: joy. It is a joy to write about: puerile and adolescent, but unafraid to shy away from real world events and intense emotions. It's a joy to read about: the stories that make up its legacy are thrilling and bizarre. It's joyful to play: energetic and barbaric, both intricate and atavistic. And of course it's a joy to listen to: to get swallowed by the chaos and emerge having confronted death face to face.

Even if you don't enjoy it, death metal contains some sort of universality: everyone is going to die. Many of us fear death, or are saddened by it in some way. We confront it every day, knowing that we are another few moments closer to the end. We find ways of dealing with personal loss, and support those who are suffering.

If death has such an enormous power, why not steel ourselves by exploring every possible outcome? The drive towards death can be empowering; by re-imagining death we humanize the experience, controlling the fear of it and reminding ourselves to enjoy the brief time we have before the inevitable.

This central tension between everything and nothing drives fans to continually want more. There are always more ways to add new elements to death metal, and there's always the ultimate nothing of death looming over us. For the enduring listener and reader, death metal is a rewarding answer to the question: *How can we celebrate the drive towards death?*

2   Death rides out (1980–9)

In the medieval morality play *Ordo Virtutum*, written circa 1151 A.D., Catholic polymath Hildegard von Bingen casts the Devil as the primary antagonist. In her notes, Hildegard directs the Devil to be played with a harsh voice, contrasting to the beautiful voices of the Virtues, pure beings of faith locked in battle over the fate of a wayward soul. One of the oldest known morality plays, *Ordo Virtutum*, is also an early surviving example of a harsh voice being used to convey dread.

'First of all, it evokes certain emotions – it makes the Devil scary and unpleasant,' says Dr Nicolete Burbach, a theologian at the London Jesuit Centre, and guitarist for Uncoffined and Nine Altars.

> However, her writing the Devil this way also has a deeper meaning – it shows his opposition to God and his opposition to the Virtues. For Hildegard, musical harmony is one part of a greater, cosmic harmony to which the world is ordered by God. She reflects this in the *Ordo Virtutum* by using singers to represent the Virtues. In contrast, by giving the Devil this harsh or grunting voice, she therefore signifies that he is opposed to the divine plan – he is not participating in the cosmic order as embodied in musical harmony. In this way, the Devil is linked to sin, enmity of virtue, and rebellion against the laws according to which God created the world.

So what does a medieval nun tell us about a band like Pig Destroyer? Perhaps that there has always been a call to express aggressive, sinister elements using a dark distortion of the voice, and that this didn't start with death metal. Similar examples exist in places as broad as Kate Bush's 1982 track 'Get Out of My House', where the singer-songwriter contorts her voice to emulate a mule in order to frighten an interloper, or the tortured wails of Chicago bluesman Howlin' Wolf, who sang of deep emotional distress.

The terrifying voice has been used to shock and frighten for generations, and as these examples show, the urge to corrupt the beauty of the voice is not an uncommon one. There is no direct link between Hildegard and Entombed, aside from illustrating how similar musical expressions have cropped up through history to denote similar themes of transgressiveness, horror and opposition to virtue.

Tempting though it is to push this point, the story doesn't start here. Instead we'll jump ahead eight centuries to the 1980s, examining death metal's foundational influences, and how the genre developed in the early years, just before its rapid expansion in the 1990s.

Collectors, distributors, fanatics

The drive to make horrifying music in modern times has been a long-running project. From proto-punks like MC5, to the shock rock of Alice Cooper, to hardcore heroes like Black Flag and Social Distortion, to the aggressive thrash bands like Slayer and Kreator, legions of musicians have hungered after the darkest, bleakest sound they could imagine. By the time the 1980s came around, these ideas had been fermenting for a long time. For many, especially in working-class communities, this was also a frightening period.

'I was terrified,' says legendary punk writer Ian Glasper, whose work includes the books *Trapped in a Scene: UK Hardcore 1985–1989* and *Burning Britain: The History of UK Punk 1980–1984*. 'I was convinced there was gonna be a nuclear war. It was a very real threat and I used to lay awake at night.'

Whilst the fear of nuclear apocalypse seems a little more distant, these conversations took place through the middle of a global pandemic, not to mention the boiling point of the climate crisis and a worrisome rise in fascism and authoritarianism around the globe. One way or another, death is at the forefront of our minds.

Glasper explains to me that the 1980s were a dark time for young musicians, and the energy that came about was channelled into aggressive underground music from across the spectrum, from technical thrash bands like Sadus to the anarchist bellowing of Crass. For younger people interested in testing boundaries, bands as diverse as this were exciting; they were straining to make music as intense and dark as possible, using wildly different techniques.

These acts were keen for more people to hear their music, just as enthusiastic listeners were excitedly searching for new dark sounds. In order to find these rare treasures, networks of deeply devoted fans developed their own complex tape trading scenes.

'The metal fanzine for me was *Metal Forces*,' Glasper remembers.

> That's how you found out about music: you picked up a fanzine and ordered a couple of tapes. You had to send a stamped envelope and 50 pence taped to a card, or a postal order that you had to buy from a post office, so it was all

really slow. You were waiting for weeks for it to come back, there were no instant purchases and emails saying it was on the way; you just wondered if they even got the money, so it built the anticipation about it arriving.

Glasper is a link to the world before record labels – with their capacities for mass production, press and distribution – would touch this aggressive music. Without labels to release and fund extreme metal acts, records and cassettes, and later CDs, were prohibitively expensive to produce on their own at a professional level. Luckily, the popularization of home tape recorders made it possible for artists and ears seeking new extremes to go around these pre-existing gatekeepers.

Using magazines as a springboard, bands and fans the world over could trade arcane demos, searching for darker material. These shoddy networks were crucial in extreme metal's early days, distributing music at low cost or for free, cataloguing obscure releases and developing a built-in fanbase for emerging bands.

'There was a tape trading scene in heavy metal going back to the early '80s,' recalls Carcass's Bill Steer. 'The older traders I knew in places like mainland Europe or the USA, they'd have all kinds of stuff, from early Iron Maiden shows from when they were still playing pubs, and demos from New Wave of British Heavy Metal bands who would later go to sign with Neat or Ebony or Heavy Metal Records.'

With ideas bouncing around their heads, impressionable kids used this network to distribute their spectacularly rough demos across cities, countries, continents and oceans. Gradually, metal fans around the world were exposed to things that would be wildly out of their wheelhouse, forcing them further and further down a road of extreme music with an increasing focus on hard, fast tunes. And those members quickly formed local connections.

'I was involved in the tape trading scene partly,' says Napalm Death vocalist Barney Greenway. 'That's how I met Shane [Embury, bass] and Mickey [Harris, drums], because they were absolutely fucking ravenous tape traders. Shane was an absolute monster, if he didn't have ten C90 cassettes coming through his letterbox every day you knew there was a breakdown in his network of friends.'

Darkness rising

With plenty of confrontational music being made around this point, a few notable acts and movements were important to anyone who was seriously looking for more extreme music.

Death metal's closest cousin was thrash metal. Thrash was speedy and engineered for excitement, with fast, distorted guitars shredding solos. In the age of Def Leppard and Mötley Crüe, bands like Slayer and Exodus were less concerned with a pristine sound as they were with pushing their performances to the next level, compelled by a youthful urge to give heavy metal more bite.

A casual reading connects the dots from early metal acts like Black Sabbath, to older NWOBHM outfits like Judas Priest, to their later, more polished cousins in Iron Maiden, to the rough and raucous thrash of Metallica, with a natural progression to death metal's extreme sounds. There is a kernel of truth here: all these bands experimented with darkness, but with thrash the gloom was distilled. This is clearly shown on the first two Metallica releases: *Kill 'Em All* (1983) cycles through songs about headbanging ('Whiplash'), playing loud ('Hit The Lights') and fighting ('Seek & Destroy'). Their sophomore effort, 1984's *Ride the Lightning*, discusses suicide ('Fade to Black') and nuclear war ('Fight Fire with Fire'). For thrash, maturity meant exploring more complex themes, if with broad strokes.

Thrash re-imagined heavy metal as grimmer and more belligerent, and as many of these bands grew in popularity, they swiftly left the underground. In doing so, they left a space for younger metal bands to soak up more influences from weirder sources, to expand on the darkness by starting from a more developed place, eschewing party anthems for the world's grim realities.

One such source was the hardcore punk scene, instrumental in popularizing a DIY attitude and a new level of aggression. In the UK, Discharge played rapid, angry music that inspired countless imitators. In America, bands like Social Distortion, Black Flag and The Dead Kennedys performed a similar role, bringing a distilled form of punk to an audience hungry for speed and fury.

These bands laid a framework for fans to grow a movement around unpalatable music, building their own distribution framework and social scene. A fascinating early example of this was a British punk band and art collective called Crass.

'I would say Crass launched the whole anarcho-punk movement,' confirms Ian Glasper. 'Without Crass there would be no Flux of Pink Indians or Subhumans or Amebix or Antisect or Icons of Filth or Conflict. Crass directly fed into all those bands. I suspect that when Napalm Death first started, they sent their demo to Crass. That's where they felt they belonged.'

In the years between 1977 and 1984, Crass ringleader Steve Ignorant and a collection of anarchists helped lead the anarcho-punk revolution in England. Advocating ideals such as animal rights, feminism and opposition to nuclear arms, they used their voice to elevate hard-line anarchist ideals of community, radical freedom and independence from government rule. They distributed flyers at their shows, organized protests and gave their albums provocative titles designed to offend. Their 1981 record, *Penis Envy*, got them banned in UK music retailer HMV and unsuccessfully prosecuted by Conservative party MP Timothy Eggar.[1] Musically, they were rough, sloppy and anthemic, but they lacked the refined edge of heavy metal, and the key vocals that would come to define death metal.

Crass are infrequently touted as a direct link to death metal; their shadow is less present in some of the early American death metal trailblazers, where much of the direct politics was phased out in favour of a focus on existential issues. Nonetheless, their DIY attitude and musical aggression helped to spark the scene. In the meantime, other forces were building, and musical movements that prioritized aggression were colliding.

'I was never a punk, but [Carcass co-founder] Jeff [Walker] was, so we were coming from two different sides of the fence,' recalls Bill Steer. 'At that point the fence was more or less being burned down anyway. It was quite exciting really. The two scenes had a lot of stuff in common but had ignored it up until that point.'

At the same time, a more sophisticated act was emerging out of Zürich, Switzerland. Formed from the ashes of black metal forefathers Hellhammer, Celtic Frost's cerebral, gothic approach to extreme metal holds up today with releases like 1984's *Morbid Tales* and 1985's *To Mega Therion*.

'*To Mega Therion* – and I don't say this about many things – is a work of genius,' Barney Greenway enthuses. 'To me it's almost like a Renaissance painting; the whole compositional entirety of that album is just genius. I can't put it any other way.'

Having something a little gloomier and more refined as a primary influence meant that bands had a different version of what they could be. The extreme metal underground was pushing itself to get darker and more complex, and the thrash that was being popularized by bands like Metallica was now warping into a richer, darker strain, fuelling the imagination of young metalheads with edgy tales of nuclear warfare, mutation and famine.

'As you discovered more of the heavier music, it almost became an obsession to find stuff that was dirtier and heavier and rawer and darker,' explains Ross Dolan, guitarist for New York death metal pioneers Immolation. 'We were really looking for darker music, from the more traditional heavy music, into the earlier thrash stuff like Slayer and even Exodus and Nuclear Assault. All that earlier thrash stuff was the foundation, and then you bring in European bands like Destruction and Kreator and Sodom that were taking thrash in a darker direction.'

But refinement wasn't everything. In 1982, NWOBHM latecomers Venom won the dark hearts of metal lovers with their second album, *Black Metal*. A disgusting mix of thrash with a grinding noise, their sound was dominating. At a time where the leading metal bands like Iron Maiden, Metallica and Megadeth were all pushing for an increasingly clean, stadium-filling sound, the record begins with a recording of dirt being shovelled onto a microphone,[2] specifically intended to freak an audience out.

'[Venom is] really interesting to write about because they had that endearing incompetence,' comments *Extreme Metal* author Keith Kahn-Harris. 'In some ways it's more interesting to read about them than actually listen to them. Some of it was really ropy.'

Venom existed on the campy side of what other bands were doing at the time. The tension between their intended effect – to flip the bird at conventional music fans – was somewhat in conflict with their goofy stage show, gleefully puerile aesthetic and over-the-top lyrics about sleeping with your schoolteacher and recording songs with Satan. Even so, no one had ever heard anything like it. Death metal certainly took some of Venom's attitude and mood, but dropped some of the immature aspects.

'I'm not sure if they were tongue-in-cheek but they certainly weren't Satanists,' Kahn-Harris quips. 'They were lads from Newcastle.'

Jumping between sophomoric humour and complex, moody music seems a little awkward in retrospect, but the variety excited young musicians at the time, and these concepts were quickly slammed together to create a mess of noises.

'It was one big melting pot of ideas,' Ian Glasper observes. 'You had American hardcore bands coming over, so you'd be listening to Sodom on the way to a gig to see Government Issues play with Napalm Death supporting. There didn't seem to be any rules and no one was analysing it, but everybody was absorbing it like a sponge.'

Ritual beginnings

Outside of this, 1984 alone saw the release of Bruce Springsteen's *Born in the U.S.A.,* Prince and the Revolution's *Purple Rain* and Madonna's *Like a Virgin.* These gorgeously produced, stadium-filling albums filled record stores and made executives fabulously wealthy.

As these records were taking shape, an extreme metal community was spreading its roots. Networks were starting to form, with bands offering favours for one another as well as sharing music. From these beginnings, the spark of new ideas – and a framework for them to be realized – had begun to sprout.

'Not until we started actively sending demos out to fanzines and tape traders did we start to really understand how vast the underground network was. That was our internet,' says Immolation's Ross Dolan. 'We had a correspondence with pretty much everybody back then who was in the scene. Most of the bands we were pen pals with were from all over the world – from South America to Europe to the States and Canada – but you had to work for it. We would spend whole evenings writing to people and sending out fan mail.'

These early experiments and pressures finally came to a head in two key locations: Birmingham, England and Tampa, Florida. Rising up from these opposing sides of the Atlantic, two bands were key to the early years of death metal: Napalm Death in the UK, and Death in the United States.

Death is a fascinating example, because their story so perfectly captures the spirit and struggle behind how death metal is made. 'He essentially kept moving because he was dedicated to the scene,' confirms Keith Kahn-Harris. 'It didn't spread from his location – the scene was wherever he was, whatever he was making happen.'

Initially calling themselves Mantas, and hailing from Florida before relocating to the San Francisco Bay Area, Death released several demos and rehearsal tapes into their tape trading networks before re-christening and unleashing their *Reign of Terror* demo into the global underground in 1984. In the meantime, inspired by similar bands, Napalm Death released the demos *Hatred Surge* in 1985 and *From Enslavement to Obliteration and Scum* in 1986. These experiments in speed and power – a mix of live tracks and rehearsal room pieces – would later be reworked into proper studio albums. But whilst both acts struggled through early lineup changes, they were beaten to the punch by Bay Area act Possessed, fronted by formidable vocalist and bassist Jeff Becerra.

Seven Churches (1985)

Released in October 1985, Possessed's debut studio full-length, *Seven Churches* is regarded as the first death metal album ever. The album opens with a low bass rumble, as Becerra's voice gurgles up like a sound from beneath the ocean, before exploding with fury. The barely legible lyrics are barked and grunted towards the listener like a punishment. Immediately the thrusting bass and grinding guitar tone are apparent. And then there's the speed; this record is desperate to be concluded as swiftly as is humanly possible, rushing headlong into a gruesome conclusion. The death metal sound had begun, with a track straightforwardly called 'Death Metal'.

'When we were branding ourselves we'd say, 'Well, Venom has black metal, Exodus and Metallica have thrash metal.' Then we said we'd call ourselves "death metal" because there's nobody using death metal,' Becerra tells me.

> Then we naively thought, 'Possessed will be known as that death metal band,' thinking we would be the only one. I never really considered the fact that people would copy it because it was a long shot to even start to think that we would get any recognition. Ninety per cent of our mindset was that we were gonna drive everybody out of the room, but we hoped they'd stay.

The key to *Seven Churches* was the terrifying vocals, which launched the death metal ship. Initially, this was a practical concern.

'We practiced super fucking loud,' Jeff Beracca tells me. 'It was so loud that you could feel it vibrate under your knees, in your feet, on your chest – the whole neighbourhood had to acquiesce to those practice sessions. You had to match vocals.'

Finally, all the darkness of metal had a focal point. *Seven Churches* means business, the sound of pissed-off kids tapping into their most primal emotions and exploding back out. It was rough, but pushing to be the best it could be, unformed but deeply passionate. Above all, Beracca's commanding voice set them apart.

'I remember the first time I sang,' Beracca recalls. 'It was super big, with a lot of reverb. After we were done I looked up and it was just me and Mike Sus (drums) and Mike Torrao (guitars) and their eyes were like saucers. I was like "is that OK?" and they're like – "yeah, yeah it's great … but it's too much. Can you tone it down just a little bit?"'

Seven Churches represented a shift in the winds, and momentum was building. Possessed proved that it was possible to take a step beyond thrash metal. Following some interest from Metal Blade, who had put them on their *Metal Massacre VI*[3] compilation in 1985 – the same series that had helped to launch Metallica – the band secured a release through Combat Records, who were most notable for working with thrash titans Megadeth. By the time the tape trading network was carrying their name overseas, the underground was ravenous for this sort of sound, providing an automatic, global audience for the band, albeit through an esoteric, hard-to-track system.

Possessed didn't last, however. After stepping away from the harsh, dark vibe they helped mint on their 1986 follow-up, *Beyond the Gates*, the band broke up by 1987. Fortunately, other bands were ready to pick up the mantle.

Season of the Dead (1987)

With Possessed's influence taking a few years to be wholly absorbed by the underground, 1987 proved to be a crucial year with a number of game-changing records, the first being February's *Season of the Dead* by Ohio band Necrophagia.

Necrophagia expanded the range of instruments, opening with sparse and sinister acoustic guitars on 'Season of the Dead', before being overtaken by an atmospheric percussive throb. Immediately, 'Forbidden Pleasure' rises up, snapping the record back into the format that Possessed established, with deathly double bass and the all-important harsh growl telling of vampires and zombies.

Season of the Dead has a sinister vibe. The double-bass playing is a key feature, not so much used to push the music forward but to really hammer home the atmosphere, acting as a bed for other instruments rather than as a constant focus to drive the action forward. With this they feel close to their cousins in thrash metal, but searching for something darker, willing to depart from conventional wisdom in order to dig deeper into the murk.

'If you go from the start of death metal, it starts off very rooted in thrash, because why throw the baby out with the bathwater? Why get rid of melodies?' says Jeff Becerra. 'Early Death, early Necrophagia, they definitely kept the thrash roots, but it wasn't that bouncy, happy thrash.'

A particular quirk of *Season of the Dead* was the influence it took from film soundtracks. Due to a general lack of extreme metal influences that evoked a sufficiently gruesome feeling, bands turned to film to study how the incidental music was specifically written to evoke a sinister or dramatic mood. Following the lead of Possessed, who covered the *Exorcist* theme on *Seven Churches*, Necrophagia went even further into this emotional space than previous metal bands had done, adding inhuman grunting on 'Ancient Slumber' to more directly emulate horror films.

With this release, death metal had direction and purpose, and excitement was starting to build. In a few short months the ideas laid out here would be taken and focused, as the movement gathered momentum.

Scream Bloody Gore (1987)

By May, a re-energized and refocused Death released their seminal first record, *Scream Bloody Gore*. Released through Combat Records, the record is immediately more technical and dramatic than what had been heard before. On their debut, the distinctions between their demos – and the work of their peers – are abundantly clear; there's a clarity of sound and ideas on this record that sets Death apart from any other major releases in this early period. Whereas Possessed sound gruesome and bassy but relatively straightforward, and Necrophagia were grainy but tried new concepts, *Scream Bloody Gore* is crisp, with clear aggressive tendencies and the all-important growl. Pitched a little lower than the style pioneered by Becerra, the vocals show frontman Chuck Schuldiner finding his signature voice.

'Me and Chuck were friends,' recalls Becerra.

> He was the first artist to really understand what we were doing. I would see Chuck and he'd be like, 'Check out this riff.' At first I just kinda brushed him off as like a fan, but then as he's sitting around and riffing, playing his B.C. Rich without

> an amp plugged in ... He really was inquisitive, getting to
> know what death metal was, because it was so obviously
> different to everything else.

With Schuldiner handling vocals, guitar and bass, the only other musician present on *Scream Bloody Gore* is drummer Chris Reifert, who formed his own band, Autopsy, that same year. As has been known to happen with pioneers, Death was initially met with total bemusement when they tried to get their ideas down.

'We went to Florida, to Chuck's parents' house, and we made an attempt to record there for the summer,' remembers Reifert.

> We went to a place called American Recording Studios.
> [The engineers] looked at us blankly, like they didn't know
> anything about metal. So we started recording there with
> just the rhythms, just the guitar and drums, and sent it to
> Combat. They heard what had been going on and said, 'No,
> this is not gonna work', so we had to scrap that plan.

It was little surprise that very few studio professionals were equipped to record this totally new sound. And in retrospect Reifert admits these early recordings lacked the recording expertise that Death were seeking. This sense of bewilderment, combined with the early issues finding personnel, was a major roadblock for Death. Such issues had been a contributing factor in Possessed's split. But, undeterred, Schuldiner and Reifert pressed on.

'[Combat] sent us to The Music Grinder in LA to do it properly. It was fucking awesome,' Reifert continues. 'It was kinda crazy as a 17-year-old, all of a sudden being in this giant studio. It felt like an airplane hangar. We got to work with Randy Burns who'd worked with Possessed. They booked a couple of teenagers hotel rooms in downtown LA and trusted us to our own devices.'

Reifert's double kick drums are a formidable, thunderous assault, but there's less focus on pure speed, particularly on tracks like 'Zombie Ritual', which features long, drawn-out riffs, and more musical space than Death's predecessors. Importantly, things flow much more on this record than for Necrophagia or Possessed; the space between the full-blooded fury of the metal elements aren't cut as harshly between the doomier, atmospheric segments. Though the record has stood the test of time, it wasn't an instant hit with the label.

'You heard so many things – "You can't understand the lyrics. You're not singing about anything important". It wasn't about politics or current events. [The album] was completely uncool at the time,' says Reifert.

> Just to solidify that point, inside the notes for *Scream Bloody Gore* it reads, 'This album is Don Kaye's folly.' Don Kaye was someone who was championing us at the time and maybe convinced Combat to sign us, but that was their disclaimer: if this flops, it's Don Kaye's fault! They put that in the fucking notes on the album. Can you imagine the nerve? We were so pissed! I still have my original copy. I scratched that out with a pen and wrote 'Fuck you!' But we prevailed in the end.

Gathering speed

These three bands were discussing death directly, and backing it up with increasingly inventive ways of musically expressing darkness. Pushing the boundaries of taste, not to mention the wisdom and patience of recording engineers, sounds like ordinary teenage things to do, but the passion to create this sort of music was manifesting throughout the world.

One of the factors that made the tape trading era so important was that it gave the bands a built-in audience when they released music; there was a whole network of people ready to devour anything heavy and dark that came their way.

'I remember talking to Daz [Darren Brookes, guitar] from Benediction about trading Death demos,' recalls Dave Hunt.

> Death were one of the earlier breakthrough acts. It felt to the guys from the early trading background that it was one of theirs that got through. Death got to the point where they sold 20,000 copies of an album or something. They would go on to sell many times that, but that was a huge milestone to all these people.

Scream Bloody Gore scratched a number of itches in the young death metal scene: it had elements of dark fantasy with tales of zombie rituals, it was fast and gloomy and it was technically advanced. Marking a significant aesthetic change over the straightforward *Seven Churches* art, one of the most important elements was the sensational artwork, depicting zombie monks drinking wine and maniacally laughing, which went a long way in igniting the imaginations of eager metal fans.

By the end of the year, the progress that the young Americans had made had started to be heard all over the world. After a few false starts, death metal had begun in earnest.

Scum (1987)

With the death metal machine now rolling in the United States, September 1987 saw a very different kind of record in the UK. Initially emerging as a sister genre to what the Americans were doing, with a similar tale of shedding members who went off to do amazing things, Napalm Death produced their debut record, *Scum*.

In 1986, having secured Napalm Death as the house band of the legendary Mermaid pub in Birmingham, owner Daz Russell convinced the band to record a single. Whilst Russell paid the studio costs, the band held onto the final recordings as retribution for unpaid dues from appearances at the Mermaid. Capturing the anarcho-punk sound of their earliest days, this became the A-side of *Scum*.

Later that year, with internal tensions running high, every member quit aside from drummer Mick Harris, the man widely suggested to be inventor of the ferocious blast beat. With a revamped lineup, they came into contact with Digby Pearson, a local promoter and founder of the newly created Earache Records, who in 1987 financed the recording of the B-side in Birmingham's Rich Bitch Studios.

Scum uses similar techniques as *Scream Bloody Gore*, particularly the rapid drums and harsh growl of both Nik Napalm and Lee Dorrian. It hints at the same darkness, but with a more scrappy approach. Though they're both concerned with death, *Scum* focused on concrete issues, discussing the perils of faceless profit in 'Multinational Corporations' and alienation in 'Human Garbage'. The tracks are extremely brief, with many tracks under a minute, and 'You Suffer' being a record-breaking highlight. Whilst the longer offerings such as 'Scum' or 'Siege of Power' are hardly odysseys, they are some of the few examples to have any kind of structure.

Scum is a morass of sounds and vibes. Whilst the American records were rudimentary, they at least had a focus. *Scum* flies in the face of this by presenting two sides that literally come from separate bands. The A-side has a raw punk feel in the vein of bands like Discharge or Crass. The B-side has a grimier metal edge, with faster guitars and a focus on greater technical proficiency. Tracks like 'Common Enemy' offer a mercilessly brief respite from the dour assault.

Somehow, it works. *Scum* sounds like someone fed up with explaining the same point to you over again about why the systems of control are so badly corrupt, losing patience and immediately getting angry about something else. It's the antithesis of the American approach, where bands pushed themselves to practise harder and more detailed material. It directly confronts the futility of existence with short bursts of fury that cry out to be howled again and again.

'You can't put your finger on it,' Ian Glasper agrees. 'If you analyse *Scum,* it shouldn't be a musical watershed moment or a timeless classic. It shouldn't be, but it is.'

Reek of Putrefaction (1988)

Following the death metal explosion of 1987, labels were opening up and presenting new opportunities for bands. The success of Napalm Death was felt across the world, with bands falling in love with Mick Harris's bizarre drumming style. Once this had been established the group quickly released their 1988 follow up, *From Enslavement to Obliteration*. Taking their speed and aggression a step further, they fortified the whirlwind style they were becoming famous for. The humour was present – as was apparent on a track like 'Cock-Rock Alienation' – but the record was presented as more than just a joke, showing how the style could be heavy, affecting and punishing.

By 1988, the UK scene had produced more outstanding bands through Earache's roster. Napalm Death guitarist Bill Steer, who also created the cover art for *Scum*, formed Carcass with bassist Jeff Walker in 1986. Released in the summer of 1988, their seminal record, *Reek of Putrefaction*, is less concerned with politics than medical conditions on standout tracks like 'Manifestation of Verrucose Urethra' and 'Carbonized Eyesockets'. On that theme, the artwork, a truly horrible collage of human and animal body parts from the deepest depths of medical textbooks, left a lastingly revolting impression.

'We wanted to poke the hornet's nest as much as possible,' Steer explains. 'When you're 17, 18, that kind of behaviour makes perfect sense. You've still got a lot of simmering resentment from school and everything. You wouldn't even be in that scene in the first place if you weren't an outsider.'

Carcass solidified death metal's obsession with gore and pathology, presenting an album that sounded just as horrible as the subject material. Faced with this music for the first time, recording engineers were baffled at how to mix it, leaving them with a record with barely any production. In the fullness of time this would go on to be considered charming, but the band were displeased with the result.

'It was a product of kids flailing around in a studio,' Steer tells me. 'We were very disappointed with the result, but it attained some notoriety just because it was so unpalatable.'

The kind of music made deliberately to perturb an audience, *Reek of Putrefaction* is the sound of a troubled teen getting way too enthusiastic about dissecting a frog. Where other bands had been punishing, this was just flatly horrible, offensive to anyone in possession of a body, and a stark reminder that after death, nothing awaits us aside from undignified decay.

Realm of Chaos (1989)

With numerous successes under its belt, Earache was on the lookout for more signings. Having released their debut *In Battle There Is No Law!* in 1988, emerging act Bolt Thrower was dissatisfied with the support from label Vinyl Solution, signing to Earache for 1989's *Realm of Chaos*. Both records focus on chaos and extreme speed, with lyrics concerning sociopolitical themes, meshed with tales and characters from the Warhammer 40,000 universe and, of course, death.

Realm of Chaos sounds like the drama of warfare distilled and bottled. The guitar riffs are primitive, with solos replaced with echoing howls, anchored by the rumble of the bass and the relentless march of the bass drums mirroring the advance of troops. With longer and more discordant tracks, Bolt Thrower showed how well-suited death metal was to capturing the horror of mass warfare.

Alongside Carcass and Napalm Death, Bolt Thrower formed a triumvirate of British extreme metal acts who would go on to direct the sound. Help was on hand from a surprisingly mainstream source in the UK. Legendary disc jockey John Peel played many of his favourite death metal bands on his show, and later invited them to record in the BBC Studios. The much-mythologized Peel Sessions were one of the first places that a lot of people heard death metal, with the mischievous DJ using his voice to amplify these voices in the same way he had elevated punk bands before. His sessions allowed bands to come in and record, and some of them were given their first recording deal off the back of that, as Bolt Thrower found out when they were approached following their first session with him. Peel even marked *Reek of Putrefaction* as his favourite release of 1988 in the widely read British newspaper *The Observer*.

'If you listened to those John Peel Sessions, like the first and second one – before I joined [Napalm Death] – the ferocity of those sessions was almost beyond comprehension,' Barney Greenway states. 'I did the third session, which also sounds fucking great. When I heard it afterwards I was laughing because it sounded so mad, so in your face!'

The Peel sessions are archived online by tireless grindcore fanatics, and were lovingly re-packaged by Earache's for the 2009 *Grind Madness at the BBC* compilation. These recordings reflect the scrappy energy of the bands and collect anecdotes such as John Peel playing 'You Suffer' multiple times in amazement, and session producer Dale Griffin's bafflement over Napalm Death's short material and aggressive play style.[4]

The sessions from Bolt Thrower, Godflesh, Extreme Noise Terror, Carcass and Napalm Death – amongst many others – have come to be considered some of the definitive editions. Incredibly, they amounted to some early financial success for the bands; Peel's initial support of *Scum* landed them the eighth slot on the UK Independent charts,[5] and *From Enslavement to Obliteration* shot them to number one, beating noise rock darlings Sonic Youth.[6]

Grinding it out

There's an interesting quirk to what some of the UK bands were doing, because the sound they helped pioneer became something adjacent to but slightly different from straight death metal. Largely confined to the deep underground, the sound from this era became known as grindcore. For bands like Bolt Thrower, Carcass and Napalm Death, the aim was to create terrifying tracks played at maximum velocity, representing a mode of aggression that is murkier, grosser and more destructive.

'I like to compare grindcore to the blues,' says filmmaker Doug Brown, director of documentary *Slave to the Grind*.

> You can have music that's bluesy but unless you actually sing about the blues it's not the blues; you can't be singing about how awesome life is – it doesn't match. If you think about the origins of grindcore, it is born out of a leftist socio-political outlook, so whereas metalheads are striving for musicianship and pushing the envelope as a writer, there's something a little more primal about grindcore, and often that will translate to a rough production and blistering speed.

The style was popular in, but not limited to Britain. *Horrified*, the sole full-length release by Michigan band Repulsion, is an early classic and a great example of Brown's point. Consisting of Death alumni Scott Carlson and Matt Olivo, *Horrified* features the bass track left over from the demo tapes due to the fact that they simply lost the studio version. The resulting muddy sound represented a significant step away from Death's polished sound.

The tension between musicianship and a search for rougher, more extreme sounds is one that's common throughout this long history, and grindcore represents the strain that embodies the desire for speed and ferocity above all else.

'Death metal is a middle finger to the world; grindcore is a middle finger to music,' Brown asserts. 'Grindcore must be fast way more than 50 per cent of the time; death metal just has to be heavy. If it doesn't have that sense of a train that's just about to go off the rails, it's not grindcore.'

All of these approaches to talking about death and horror are valid ways of dealing with the oncoming infinity of death, with modern bands such as Wallowing writing noise-drenched interstellar concept albums or Atomçk diving deep into Britain's miserable austerity politics. But defining the rough shape of grindcore gives death metal more distinction. The tension between the two – solely interested in upsetting people, or noise without focus – is a vision of what death metal could have become. Whereas the story of grindcore is one of wild boundary-pushing, with stunning acts such as Discordance Axis, Insect Warfare and Full of Hell, it's also one of near-total obscurity. Unlike death metal, which was about to gain bizarre success by adding more shape and definition to its sound, grindcore remained resolutely opposed to any such structure.

Whilst death metal's dark shadow was developing, the scene was quickly developing in America. Just as the rough voice was favoured by medieval nuns looking to add a sinister edge to a cautionary tale, it was slowly winning fans over as bands harnessed their scattered influences to stare death straight in the face.

3 Death rising (1988–93)

At the 1992 BRIT Awards, in front of a crowd of music journalists, UK acid house act The KLF appeared alongside grindcore's finest, Extreme Noise Terror, to perform a version of their hit '3 a.m. Eternal'. The rendition they played took the layered synths of the original and mangled them beyond belief, ending up with a version that was extremely noisy, and *extremely* terrifying. As the legend goes, The KLF had wanted to spray pig's blood into the crowd, but our boisterous heroes, being concerned with animal rights, objected.

In dark corners of the earth, meanwhile, death metal festered. Spreading like tendrils, the movement was gathering momentum, and by the start of the 1990s, the voracity of the earlier bands had inspired legions of fanatics. Through the wide network of tape trading, and more recently specialist labels, bands were starting up who would take the darkness of death metal and mould it in their image.

'When death metal first came out, I thought it was a refreshing new genre of music. It made complete sense to me. It was the heaviest thing I'd ever heard, but it was also really, really good,' says Metal Blade's Brian Slagel, 'When Slayer and Metallica came out, that was the heaviest thing ever, and eventually that became mainstream, right? I just knew that that was gonna happen to death metal. The music was so good and so cool, it was only a matter of time before it was gonna get really popular.'

The early 1990s would be the era of classic albums and genre-defining giants like Morbid Angel, Deicide, Cannibal Corpse and Obituary, representing the single fastest advancement in death metal's history.

Severed Survival (1989)

Over in America, Chuck Schuldiner had moved around enough times to create multiple mini-scenes, as the number of ex-Death members starting their own bands grew in his wake. The most notable example was Autopsy, which Chris Reifert formed in 1987 after Chuck moved Death back to Florida, parting ways with his drummer. With their 1989 debut *Severed Survival*, Autopsy harnessed the ponderous elements from doom metal to make something gruesome and moody, setting a standard for death metal bands who were looking for a broader emotional punch.

'There was a whole bunch of slow stuff we liked: Trouble, Saint Vitus, Candlemass, Witchfinder General, Pentagram,' Reifert tells me. 'At that time there weren't that many bands playing that sort of style, but we liked them all along with the fast stuff like Terrorizer, Slayer and Master. In terms of playing we just wanted to be heavy.'

Compared to a few years prior, when studios didn't know what to do with this new sound, there was a palpable difference in the ease of recording. The band went to Starlight Sound under the guidance of producer and engineer John Marshall, finding a notably smoother experience than recording *Scream Bloody Gore*. For one thing, Autopsy had a whole contingent of members; more than could be said for the two-piece unit of Schuldiner and Reifert on Death's debut. But the experience wasn't without its barriers, some of them self-imposed.

'We did something that we didn't tell Peaceville at the time: we got a budget of $5,000 for the album and we spent half of it on weed,' Reifert confesses. 'That left us with four days to make the record, so we had to do it really fast. It left us very little room for error, so we had to turn up and know exactly what to do, with very few overdubs.'

Severed Survival is the soundtrack to a hack surgeon operating on you, then slowly offering the mirror so you can gaze on your new adjustments. The musical answer to classic tales such H.P. Lovecraft's 'Herbert West – Reanimator', the gloomy passages give shape to the riffs, heightening the claustrophobia before the faster sections pummel the listener into sticky oblivion.

By this point the scene was starting to develop elders – bands like Napalm Death, Carcass and Death who were already on their second or third album. Many of the bands who had come from the grindcore scene were becoming more focused on musicianship as their abilities developed. Carcass's sophomore record, *Symphonies of Sickness,* for example – released on Earache in December 1989 – represented a significant step up in sound quality from the borderline-unlistenable first offering.

'I love thinking about the progression of the first three Carcass albums,' muses respected metal producer Colin Marston. 'Just going from something where nobody knew what the hell to do with that sound to having the second album be, in comparison, a crystal clear studio product. And now it's looked at as a very lo-fi rough recording.'

They weren't the only act tightening up. By this point, engineers were getting used to the new sound, and bands were starting to push away from the technical issues that had dogged them.

Morrisound

Ever striving to push the envelope, bands were looking for a sound that would challenge their listeners whilst clarifying their ideas. Just as Autopsy had enjoyed a better recording experience, other bands were finding opportunities opening for them.

It was the perennial trailblazers in Death who drew people to the next step, and the nexus ended up being in Florida, where Chuck Schuldiner had relocated the band following *Scream Bloody Gore*. Re-forming with new members, Death's restless toiling in the studio led to the release of *Leprosy* in 1988 and *Spiritual Healing* in 1990.

Leprosy retains some of the gloomy, sinister vibes of its predecessor. The playful, ringing guitars provide the bulk of the melody as Schuldiner's haunting voice spins relentlessly bleak tales of disease and banishment, snaking around the pacy drums that drive everything forward. But by the time *Spiritual Healing* emerged two years later, the ideas were a lot more fleshed out. The snare was clearer and the vocals were cleaner, allowing the ideas more space to breathe. When the weirdly-phased solos on 'Living Monstrosity' hits, it brings with it an otherworldly feeling that's absent on the rougher early recordings.

Both records, albeit with different lineups, were steps forward in technicality and ferocity. Crucially, they were the first of the death metal crowd to feature the crisper sound of producer Scott Burns, who quickly became a key player in the Florida scene. As a result of *Leprosy* and *Spiritual Healing's* success, more artists began to migrate to Tampa's Morrisound Recording Studios in search of a more intelligible sound.

It's helpful to get a technical sense of how this sound appeared, which Colin Marston was kind enough to help demystify.

'To me there's two Morrisound sounds,' he says.

> There's the Morris sound – Tom and Jim Morris were the other engineers, they did the Morbid Angel records – and then there's Scott Burns, who did everything else. He did most of the Death records, and the early Cannibal Corpse, Cynic, and Atheist records. When I think of Scott I think of the guitar sound, which was the Marshall Valvestate, the Ampeg VH-150C with bass on 10, treble on 10, mids on 0, and maybe more mids scooping in the mix. To me that's the Scott Burns sound.

What Marston is describing here is the guitars that sit a little higher in the mix, with very little bass presence. Meanwhile, the bass drum is also more distinct, instead of being a low throb. This helps to define some of the instruments, a process that was developed rapidly in Burns's early efforts, and there's a very distinct difference in the two Death records recorded under him. And once other bands had cottoned on, many of them flocked there.

This approach wasn't beloved by all. It was an earnest attempt to capture the horror of the subject matter and the mortifying death growl, whilst dealing with musicians who were wildly talented. But to some, striving for such clarity was counterproductive to death metal's transgressive aims.

'Growing up, I hated it,' Marston admits.

> To me it was sacrificing pitch for rhythm. They had this great heavy palm mute tone but whenever there was a tremolo

riff or something where they weren't palm muting it just sounded like noise. Over the years my ear has developed and gotten more comfortable with death metal, but as a kid it was really shocking and harsh, and just kinda dingy and bad. Like, why would you mix something this way? But now I'm like, 'Oh yeah, he was figuring this shit out.'

Altars of Madness (1989)

Altars of Madness is the sound of being hunted through forgotten tombs by diseased ghouls, slowly shedding the last rags of your sanity. Death metal is weird, but Morbid Angel are a cut above. Stories of their exploits are etched into death metal apocrypha: like drummer Pete Sandoval passing out in a pool of his own sweat after practising playing double bass as fast as he can, or guitarist Trey Azagthoth's flat-out demented musicianship, taking the guitar and making it wail as if it were being slowly melted.

Morbid Angel were an early adopter of the Morrisound studio before the Scott Burns sound became the standard. Moving to Florida from Charlotte, North Carolina in 1988, they released their debut, *Altars of Madness*, the following year. Like other records of the time, the album sounds raw and primitive, but there were some major advancements too.

For one, the songs sounded a lot more coherent. Tracks like 'Maze of Torment' and 'Suffocation' are fast-paced and ferocious, with something even resembling a hook. The focus of the record was speed, exercising a ridiculous capacity for velocity comparable to the wilder moments of Napalm Death's early work. The double kick drums and snare sounds are crisper and clearer than the clumsy approach of other bands.

Altars of Madness's secret weapon, however, is that it is also bewilderingly strange, crafting awkward and chaotic tales of madness that tap into the same well as H.P. Lovecraft. The album's matching cover art, drawn by the great death metal illustrator Dan Seagrave, depicts screaming souls, contorted in a more abstract manner than many of their friends and rivals.

Elsewhere on *Altars of Madness*, the elements seen before are tighter, with a particular build on the blast beat. Here, it is not used continuously, but scattered around to punctuate specific moments. It's not just about tempos either; there are plenty of elements that hadn't featured before in death metal. Notable experiments – like David Vincent's deep intonations on 'Immortal Rites', and the creepy synthy passages on 'Chapel of Ghouls' – reveal the band's vision to create not just a capital-H horrible record but something that cuts a little deeper.

'The Morbid Angel records are all super weird,' Marston tells me flatly.

> They're all super different from each other, and from their peers. I think you can chalk a lot of that up to Trey Azagthoth just being a genuine weirdo genius. He's an incredibly talented dude who's super into being unique and not following anyone else's trends. His favourite guitar player is Eddie Van Halen. Does Morbid Angel sound anything like Van Halen? Not even his solos sound like Eddie!

Slowly We Rot (1989)

Slowly We Rot is the sound of being smashed to pieces by hammers, dropping the scalpel precision in favour of blunt trauma. It's concussive cascade of dull blows to the cranium and upper torso, a remorseless assault against the senses and the body.

As Morbid Angel were taking a leftfield approach, bands like Obituary were rising through the ranks with more grounded sensibilities. Dropping in 1989, their Scott Burns-produced debut, *Slowly We Rot*, is a slower, groovier take on the genre, forged on the relentless hammer blows of the double kick technique, which sent waves through the whole aesthetic of death metal. Bringing these driving, dramatic and ferocious drums to the forefront, the Morrisound approach filtered out impurities to crystallize a classic.

Whereas bands like Death presented a more varied picture in their early work, the new breed of more brutal bands formed a harsh, pummelling bedrock on which everything else could be layered. On *Slowly We Rot,* Obituary leant into a gloomier sound, with stabs of melody piercing through the thick sludge of guitars. Tracks like 'Internal Bleeding' assault the listener, proving that the genre could evolve to something less shiny and bright while being just as musically crushing.

Much like Autopsy did on *Severed Survival*, Obituary showed that death metal could be slow and driving instead of constantly operating at breakneck speed. This departure from grindcore further carved out a death metal sound that wasn't dependent on quickness so much as vibe.

Deicide (1990)

Deicide sounds like a journey into hell, as demons claw at your feeble limbs on your descent. Benton's vocals are pure evil, and there's a transgressive thrill of blasphemy that elevates them above much from this era. Fearlessly railing against organized religion, the album leans hard into the spectacularly forceful blast beat, separating it from the rest of the sound so the guitar riffs had more space to breathe.

The year 1990 marked the introduction of Deicide, a band whose wild history includes some of the more authentically repulsive tales in death metal lore. One story goes that vocalist and bassist Glen Benton stormed into the office of Roadrunner Records, threw his demo tape at A&R man Monte Connor, and verbally berated him. They were signed within a week.[1]

In the meantime, Deicide preoccupied with carving a niche as being a particularly gruesome live band, causing them to pull stunts like filling mannequins with viscera from butcher shops and having Benton brand an inverted crucifix into his forehead.[2] Later, in 1992, Benton paused an interview with the *NME* to shoot a troublesome squirrel with an air rifle, which earned him serious disdain from animal rights groups. Reportedly, they were behind the planting of bombs at the Manchester and Stockholm stops of their *Legion* tour.[3]

Before such events had escalated, they were a hardworking unit. Having released a handful of demos under the names of Amon and Carnage going back to 1987, they re-titled as Deicide – meaning 'the killing of a god' – in time to drop their self-titled debut.

Deicide were distinctly blasphemous, which leaked into every pore of their being. Unlike records that were concerned with human suffering or bodily decay, the track *Deicide* literally threatens Jesus Christ with death if he was to rise again. In terms of transgressiveness, not much can top that.

And though few would accuse Deicide of having pop sensibilities, there was something fun and catchy about them. This is in part thanks to Benton's vocals; individual words are barked out, retaining the evil vibe, and the staccato delivery builds tension before breaking it back down with chaotic guitar solos.

Deicide is an example of how death metal refined the nasty edge of grindcore but retained a sinister sound. A cornerstone of this record is its brutal brevity, with tracks rarely breaching the 2-to-3-minute mark. The structure of the tracks is rarely based around a solid verse-chorus structure but generally features tighter songwriting than their contemporaries. Everyone I spoke to had something to say about Deicide, notably about how memorable the tracks were.

'Part of the challenge is writing a song that is catchy without it sounding poppy,' Chase Mason explains. 'My reference for that is always Cannibal Corpse or Deicide.'

Eaten Back to Life (1990)

Mason's other example represents the peak of death metal's body horror obsession. When Cannibal Corpse turned their revolting eye to the genre, they infused it with a horror movie repulsion and amped it up a hundred times.

Eaten Back to Life is a bellicose record with a percussion that emulates the relentless pound of meat hammers in the abattoir, the soundtrack to a serial killer's abhorrent lair. With the sonic standard by now set, the band leant much further into the heavy double bass and palm muting that would define the genre.

Of the myriad styles that emerged in this time, Cannibal Corpse's was the least subtle. Formed in Buffalo, New York in 1988, but soon relocating to Florida to record, the band quickly attracted the attention of Metal Blade Records, who released their debut, *Eaten Back to Life,* in 1990.

'I looked at the [demo] tape and there was a song on there called "A Skull full of Maggots",' Brian Slagel tells me. 'I said "I don't care what this sounds like, I'm gonna sign them based on that song title alone."'

Thematically they explore the fantastical universe of horror, parading a revolting fascination with the human body in the vein of Carcass, but with a vividly cinematic perspective. Tracks like 'Edible Autopsy', 'Shredded Humans' and 'Bloody Chunks' had a more puerile sensibility than Carcass, who were approaching their material at least partially from the perspective of human and animal rights concerns. Cannibal Corpse, on the other hand, chose to dedicate their album to the memory of early American cannibal Alferd Packer.

Death over the world

The staggering array of sounds and viewpoints that this period hatched would all go on to mould death metal's sound. They were all discussions of the numerous forms of death, all trying to perturb an audience that was quickly growing attached to a harsh, challenging sound, and who were keen to see what else the genre could throw at their increasingly calcifying sensibilities.

Soon people from far outside Florida were making a special pilgrimage to Morrisound.

'To know that Deicide, Death, Morbid Angel, and all those bands were in that studio was a super amazing experience,' says Suffocation's Terrance Hobbs. 'Florida was a big thing; that was like our central hub or Mecca. For us to go down to Morrisound, recording with Scott Burns, an amazing engineer, was just unbelievable.'

Well beyond the borders of Florida, this detonation led to an explosion of interest and an increasingly diverse set of approaches.

A new wave of bands in the UK were expanding their pool of influences, drawing on the murky fens and bogs, and Gothic film and literature. By the early 1990s, bands like Paradise Lost, Anathema and My Dying Bride all found a home with the fledgling British label Peaceville Records, and established themselves as slower and doomier projects, leaning into the naturally eerie aura of the Northern landscape. Alongside seminal bands like Winter, the style later came to be known as death-doom, taking its name from the ponderous doom metal of bands like Trouble, Saint Vitus and Pentagram, not to mention the early roots of Black Sabbath.

'If you listen to early Anathema, the lyrics are forlorn, lovelorn,' says Kat Shevil Gillingham, who has written for magazines like *Terrorizer*, and plays for Uncoffined, Thronehammer and Nine Altars. 'Paradise Lost had that similar grim approach. You don't get more downtrodden than "Rotting Misery" or "Lovelorn Rhapsody". So I think a lot of the doom-death bands definitely put the emphasis on misery, grief, depression, and all-out darkness and morbidity.'

The early 1990s also saw mainland Europe, and in particular Scandinavia, waking up to the death metal sound. In Sweden, bands like Stockholm's Entombed, whose cutting guitar tone was played through the merciless Boss HM-2 pedal, helped to define an aesthetic that was largely devoid of melody. However, there were numerous strands of death metal developing in this Nordic realm. The general way of thinking splits the Swedish sound into two camps.

'If you listen to a lot of the Stockholm bands it's very punky in places,' Gillingham explains. 'On the flipside of that you have the Gothenburg death metal, which is a lot more melodic.'

Gothenburg boasted bands like At the Gates, who would go on to define a guitar sound that leant towards melody and away from the brutal sound of their compatriots. With a cultural acceptance of kids starting metal bands, and government-funded practice spaces, bands worked hard on their craft and gave one another space to develop creatively, and the scenes flourished.

'In those days we didn't see it as different scenes in the cities,' says At the Gates vocalist Tomas Lindberg.

> There were so few bands, it didn't matter that Grave were from Gottland or Nihilist were from Stockholm. We were so young – 14, 15, 16 – that on summer holidays you took the train and spent the week at a penpal's house when they still lived at home. If we wanted to meet other bands like us, we had to arrange shows or go play a local show that they arranged in youth clubs and squats.

Not too far away, bands in Finland were making further adjustments to the sound.

'I always thought it was really cool that the Finnish scene was really different sounding to the Swedish scene, even though the countries are next to each other,' notes Gillingham. 'Finnish death metal was darker and more morbid-sounding generally, as well as being quite quirky. Bands like Disgrace had a bit of a bounce and a groove to them, but they still had the Finnish morbidity and darkness, whereas the Swedish bands were a more straight ahead HM-2 chainsaw attack, and very punky in their approach.'

On another border, Norwegian acts were pursuing a darker path. Darkthrone presented *Soulside Journey* to the world in 1990 and Old Funeral released a handful of demos before 1991's *Devoured Carcass* EP. These offerings were murky, but showed new bands straining to tighten their sound. As history would unfold, these bands would go on to create a dark parallel to death metal, but their early efforts followed a similar pattern to bands across Europe and America.

States of decay

As Europe was opening up to death metal, these albums trickled out through newly formed labels and fed back into America, where bands were finding the darkness in their own backyards, including death metal heavyweights Immolation, who emerged from the New York City suburb of Yonkers.

'There's a lot of darkness attached to Yonkers,' confirms bassist and vocalist Ross Dolan. 'In the '70s I remember the Son of Sam killings. We did a lot of our early photos at the park that was implicated in those murders, so we knew about that dark, seedy history.'

With more and more records coming out, tape trading was still flourishing, and bands used it as an active tool to make more connections and seed the community around them.

'It was like an assembly line,' Dolan recalls. 'We would be on Bob's [Vigna, guitars] dining room table all night, and we'd sit down and write to everybody. We had a million of those little flyers. You were not only promoting your band but all the other bands who you had corresponded with.'

Showing that labels were also catching on, Immolation's 1991 debut, *Dawn of Possession*, was released on Roadrunner

Records. Also from the New York scene came Suffocation and Incantation, who both signed deals in 1990, with Suffocation releasing their legendary debut *Effigy of the Forgotten* in 1991. Rather than following trends, these bands were forging their own paths, despite some early factionalism.

'We have a hardcore influence in us as well as a metal influence,' Terrance Hobbs tells me. 'It was almost like a warring effort: skinheads vs longhairs. It was kinda fucked up.'

Harmony Corruption (1991)

By 1991, the allure of Florida brought some bands in from as far away as the UK to the Sunshine State.

'We never wanted to emulate that whole death metal thing. We just went to Morrisound because we were looking for a different type of sound,' says Napalm Death's Barney Greenway.

> The band members were kind of against it at first, but Earache kind of sold it to us like, 'What are you talking about? You're gonna get four weeks in Florida.' For people who came from working class backgrounds, we never would have had a hope of going to a place like that aside from the band. So when we went to Morrisound, [the media] said, 'Oh that's it, Napalm is a death metal band now.'

Released by Earache in 1991, Napalm Death's third album, *Harmony Corruption* – their first with Greenway as vocalist – was a departure from their earlier work. Whereas *From Enslavement to Obliteration* is slipshod, *Corruption* makes a clear effort to be structured, naturally bringing their style closer to the bands in the Florida scene. Choice cut 'Suffer the Children' is a notable example, adding a tighter architecture to their berserk style. On top of that, Obituary's John Tardy and Deicide's Glen Benton add an extra splash of Tampa magic by providing guest vocals on 'Unfit Earth'.

Harmony Corruption is a heavy record with cuts that are performed live to this day. But despite an excellent showing from newcomer Greenway, whose rough bark adds some gruff to the deeply political lyrics, it lacks the unhinged madness of Napalm's earlier records, and thus a little of the boundary-pushing spark is dulled.

'Personally it wasn't what I wanted from Napalm Death at all', recalls Keith Kahn-Harris. 'You could argue that one of the things that happened with death metal is that the challenge that it presented got a bit domesticated.'

What Kahn-Harris outlines here is a narrative that would come to dog many a death metal band trying to grow as artists: the accusation that it was losing its edge by taking on a more coherent tone. Following *Harmony Corruption*, Napalm Death underwent some lineup changes, including losing their trademark drummer, Mick Harris. While tracks from this record are still played live to this day, and they would go on to have what Kahn-Harris calls an 'incredible renaissance', the muted reception of *Harmony Corruption* represents the growing pains of death metal in its adolescent phase.

Kicking back

This was the first crack in death metal's armour. Even so, things were going surprisingly well on the business side.

Death metal was never enormously lucrative, but sales were climbing, thanks in part to unlikely mainstream champions. John Peel's Napalm Death session propelled the band into the spotlight, and following their first session with him, rapid sales forced a hurried re-press,[4] and shone a spotlight on the other bands on the Earache roster.

Financial success was encouraged by MTV's *Headbanger's Ball*, which broadcast extreme metal music videos to the masses, giving fans access to the freshest offerings and providing unsuspecting people a space to stumble across the music. This was a huge boon to developing bands and labels, driving record sales and showcasing their strongest material. Notable videos such as Morbid Angel's 1993 *God of Emptiness* promo were featured on *Beavis and Butt-Head*, rubbing shoulders with the likes of Nirvana's *Smells Like Teen Spirit*, advertising them to a much wider audience.

Tracking album sales is a slippery business, and Nielsen Soundscan began tracking album sales in 1991, just after some of these records were released. They list Deicide's debut as having sold over 100,000 copies to date.[5] For context, the current best-selling record of all time, Michael Jackson's *Thriller*, has sold in excess of 66 million copies.[6] For bands who trade on tunes about serial killers, blasphemous rituals and eating human flesh, those aren't dreadful numbers.

This wasn't all positive, and bands that were courting controversy for smaller audiences soon found themselves coming up against more severe pushback. Following the release of *Severed Survival*, for instance, Autopsy found resistance to Kent Mathieu's provocative cover art, which illustrated a fleshy human torso being torn apart by meathooks.

'Peaceville heard some distributors wouldn't take it because the art was too gory, too graphic, so they asked us how we'd feel about getting alternative cover art,' says Chris Reifert.

Autopsy got away with the censors, label and band unperturbed, but other bands faced a fiercer revolt. On their albums *Butchered at Birth* (1991) and *Tomb of the Mutilated* (1992), Cannibal Corpse expanded their fascination with the human body to explore the female form in gruesome fashion, as evidenced with song titles such as 'Stripped, Raped and Strangled', 'Fucked with a Knife' and 'Entrails Ripped Through a Virgin's Cunt'. Due to their highly offensive lyrics and artwork, the band's music was banned in both Australia and Germany, and to this day they are unable to perform tracks such as 'Born in a Casket', with its lyrics about impregnating a dead body, in the latter country.

'With Cannibal Corpse there were times in Europe that were really scary, to the point where the local government said if they played their songs then we would arrest them immediately,' says Brian Slagel.

> We were told that if we have any of the albums in our office, they would arrest the guy running the office. They're also banned in Korea. At one point in Korea they had to translate all the lyrics into Korean, and the lyrics were like 'Oh, roses and nice things'. Eventually the person who did that at the label we licensed it to ended up in jail for like a year.

The most harrowing example of active censorship was the 1991 raid on Earache Records, whose offices were invaded by UK police over the back cover of the Painkiller record, *Guts of a Virgin*, which featured a black-and-white photo of a woman being dissected to reveal a foetus.

Under the UK's Obscene Publications Act, the record was seized at the airport and the offices were ransacked, with the police confiscating valuable stock of CDs and LPs, as well as a large poster of Alice Cooper holding a severed head. Operating under a strange and oblique definition of 'offensive', Dismember's 1991 album, *Like an Everflowing Stream*, also came under fire due to the track 'Skin Her Alive'.

Death Metal

The charges were eventually dropped, and the setback didn't stop Earache or anyone else from trading.[7]

While death metal would continue to stir controversy over the years, Western government interference had limited success, and frequently backfired by adding to the mystique of this loud and revolting music. The Recording Industry Association of America instituted their infamous 'Parental Advisory' stickers for offensive content in 1985, specifically targeting hip-hop and metal artists. Aside from exciting fans with the promise of something forbidden, it seems a little redundant to apply this sticker to a record such as *Tomb of the Mutilated*, which depicts two corpses engaged in cunnilingus.

Jumping ahead, a similar instance occurred in 1995 where Republican presidential candidate Bob Dole publicly announced his disdain for Cannibal Corpse, claiming their depictions of mindless violence were an unfit influence on the youth of America. In addition to raising their profile, an aide later confirmed that he had not listened to the band, depriving them of at least one fan.[8]

'Censorship is a fun cage to be trapped in because of the pathetically easy way that it can be transgressed,' says metal philosopher David Burke. 'All you have to do is find ten dollars and go to a record shop on your own when your mum isn't looking, and that's how you beat the game. It's a cute jail; it makes you feel like you're breaking out of something but really it was woefully ineffective.'

Perils of death

Government interference in metal wasn't always a laughing matter. Metal bands around the globe have faced censorship from police and authority figures over the years. Voices

I interviewed told of interference from Russian authorities, and police following longhaired metal fans in South America.

Animosity between these groups wasn't the only early issue for the global spread of death metal. To the surprise of no-one, there were some territories that were especially resistant to such outlandish noise, and where performing it was outright dangerous.

For example, 1991 saw the release of *Arise* by Brazilian group Sepultura. Closer to the thrash style than many of the American acts, the grimy grunt of Max Cavalera gave them a particularly subterranean aesthetic. Recorded with Scott Burns at Morrisound, they pushed the style into new, experimental directions by adding Latin percussion and industrial flourishes.

The record proved popular, and they played a show in São Paulo's Praça Charles Miller, just outside of Pacaembu Stadium, for an unexpectedly large crowd. Eyewitness accounts estimated 40,000 concertgoers, far outstripping the 10,000 which the open-air venue could comfortably hold. Eventually, in a drunk and riotous mood, the crowd got out of hand, and several people were injured in the ruckus – one fatally, sparking a media backlash against the genre, the band and rock music in general.

In stark contrast to places like Sweden, where government funding actively supported band, the realities were a little harsher for a band like Polish legends Vader. The turn of the 1990s was a fraught time for Eastern Europe, and the band fought for nearly a decade to get heard before releasing their debut, *The Ultimate Incantation*, on Earache in 1992. The record flits between disquieting atmospheres and pitiless guitar spectacle, but making music in Poland presented some difficulties.

'The problem was that we were living behind the Iron Curtain, so everything was a bit delayed,' says Vader vocalist and bassist Piotr Wiwczarek. 'We just had to work twice as hard to get where we wanted to get. We wanted to play to escape from the realities of Poland in the '80s and '90s, which were pretty dark, or grey and boring. Even if we had to use handmade or shit equipment, we just did it, and people understood it.'

Both Sepultura and Vader are volatile and unpredictable examples of death metal fortitude, and speak to the passion of making art against the odds. But even when bands had reliable studios and safer performance venues, hardships presented themselves.

These battles would rage on. Despite its ever-presence, death is a touchy subject, and for outsiders, death metal's colourful presentation can seem crass, disrespectful or even blasphemous. Over the next period, internal tensions tightened, threatening the hard-won victories for the movement, and casting doubt over its future.

4 Deathly peaks (1993–6)

A man with a stiff quiff stalks across the sweaty music venue. The air drips with perspiration, his thin shirt hanging limp from his lanky frame. He needs answers. He tries to speak with a small group of oblivious headbangers – they fail to notice him over the thunder of the band, who're busy grunting repugnant tales of grime and horror. Buffeted by the moshpit, he retreats to safety as crowd surfers fly overhead.

Ace Ventura: Pet Detective hit cinemas across the world in 1994. At the behest of star Jim Carrey – a fan of the genre, and Cannibal Corpse in particular – the filming schedule was rearranged so that the band could appear in a scene set at a death metal concert. In a deleted scene, Ace even evades a pair of in-pursuit captors by crowd surfing, then stripping his shirt off to scream with the band, causing such a ruckus that his would-be assailants are swept away by the tides. The cameo of course ballooned Cannibal Corpse's popularity, adding a whole bunch of young fans who could appreciate the humour. The film's lasting popularity has even led many fans to wear Hawaiian shirts and quiffs to their concerts, a stark contrast to the black shirt and combat shorts of their usually dour crowds.

For all the controversies, death metal was finding allies in unusual places. And as it came into the mid-1990s, fuelled by a fast turnover of established bands producing new records, the genre was getting more attention than ever. As stories like the above show, death metal bands found themselves on the right side of a set of changing attitudes for the decade.

'I think there's a wider musical trend that hit different music scenes in the '90s, but particularly metal, which was a tendency to want authenticity. I think that's part of the challenge that grunge represented,' Keith Kahn-Harris states. 'A lot of longstanding metal bands, like Judas Priest and Iron Maiden, had very fallow years in the '90s. Other bands like Metallica had some of that grungy feeling but without knowing quite how to do it.'

Leading up to this, 1991's *Nevermind* had shown that bands like Nirvana could re-write what a mainstream hit could sound and look like. As they were shepherding grunge into the spotlight, Metallica released their self-titled 1991 record. Bringing a version of heavy metal to a wider audience, this was an easy point entry for metal newcomers who only had to dig a little deeper to find a harsher sound. A more mainstream appeal saw them shedding some of their older fans, driving them to seek out the dulcet tones of death metal, which only deepened as their style moved away from thrash metal into the 1990s and beyond. Extreme bands that seemed permanently destined for the underground found a whole new audience.

The hunt for authenticity that Kahn-Harris notes was a contributing factor behind death metal's success. It was clearly heartfelt, earnest and the successes it enjoyed did not come as a result of any major compromises. It presented the unfiltered vibe of grunge for an audience that craved a harder sound.

In terms of business, bands found themselves staring down opportunities beyond their wildest dreams: after a few rounds of financial success, major labels were willing to take a risk.

Established bands, meanwhile, were touring to an expanding audience and enjoying the fruits of their labours.

'When our third album came out, it ended up selling really well,' Chris Reifert recalls of Autopsy's 1992 album, *Acts of the Unspeakable*. 'I remember [Peaceville Records founder Paul "Hammy" Halmshaw] saying "This record sold more than we thought it would! We don't have the money all at once to pay you, but can we spread it over the year in increments", and we were like "Yes!" We were able to live on that album pretty much for a year.'

Tightening up

Though death metal songwriters weren't moving away from the grim subject material, there was a growing desire for clarity, with bands tightening up to better communicate weird or abstract ideas of death, and to court some of the more lucrative commercial possibilities. This more professional approach, forged from recording engineers and musicians working to refine the sound, would be the spark that finally ignited the interest of larger organizations.

'Within the confines of that genre there's always a tension: where do you go with extreme music? What limits are left to explore?' says Keith Kahn-Harris. 'One of the reasons I think that some extreme metal artists end up producing more technical or more listenable work is because ultimately it becomes less artistically satisfying to produce that kind of [unsophisticated] stuff. I don't think many people are capable of that level of obsession, to explore this very narrow furrow for an indefinite period of time.'

Individual Thought Patterns (1993)

The trajectory that Kahn-Harris describes was commanded by Death. With a totally new lineup, adding guitarist Paul Masvidal, bassist Steve Di Giorgio and drummer Sean Reinert, they had released *Human* in 1991, before swiftly swapping in Andy LaRocque on guitar and Gene Hoglan on drums for 1993's *Individual Thought Patterns*.

Tracking the changes in Death lineups can be exhausting, but those two records are especially different. *Human* is staggeringly complex, opening with a cascade of tom fills on 'Flattening of Emotions' and evolving to the otherworldly instrumental 'Cosmic Sea', where neoclassical guitars delicately dance around in tension with the deep throb of the percussion. By contrast, *Individual Thought Patterns* is significantly more intense, moving away from the jazz fusion style and back to a heavy double bass assault. Retaining the bizarre technical twists, tracks like 'Overactive Imagination' stop on a dime to throw some surprising percussive flourishes in, and 'The Philosopher', which discusses differences in perception, is punctuated by Chuck Schuldiner's sceptical howl.

Individual Thought Patterns sounds like everything you thought you knew about dying re-arranged into something newly horrifying. The record uses technicality as a weapon, summoning arcane flashes to shock and surprise dedicated listeners.

'Death and Chuck found the thin line between writing extremely progressive and intense songs, but staying memorable. There are hook lines in all the songs,' says Obscura guitarist Steffen Kummerer. 'I still try to follow this path, combining the progressive elements and establishing structures you can follow, so you appeal to fans who are not musicians. Someone who is going to a show and having a beer with friends can have a good time as well.'

Heartwork (1993)

Heartwork is the sound of horror taking on a new form. Just as the death growl warps the voice beyond comprehension, guitar melodies that might inspire or uplift in other contexts are twisted and corroded.

Death weren't the only band who were pushing their own boundaries. On Carcass's third album, 1991's *Necroticism – Descanting the Insalubrious*, the band embraced a more straightforward death metal sound, comparable to Napalm Death's adjustment. But by their fourth release, 1993's *Heartwork*, they had moved away from their hideous phase into something significantly more melodic. They also improved significantly as musicians and flexed their muscles with longer and more complex songs.

Rather than treating them as assault weapons, tracks like 'Heartwork' showed more thoughtful engagement with instruments, with more distinctive riffs and guitar harmonies that owe as much to Thin Lizzy as they do to Death. The melodies are downright fun while lyrically dipping back into body horror, blasphemy and tales of bodily decay and mass graves.

With this new development, Carcass were marking themselves out in a crowded field.

'I wouldn't say there was a huge thought process as such. It was more of a natural development,' Bill Steer recalls.

With *Symphonies*, that's the peak of our 'extreme' period, where we were still fully up for making music that was totally nihilistic. Around that period quite a few other bands started to surface who were operating in similar territories, and without even needing to discuss it we just knew that we wanted to go elsewhere. It just does something to you; your identity is getting swallowed up, and some of us wished to stand apart to some degree.

No longer just seeking the thrill of controversy, Carcass were stretching beyond the boundaries of their musicianship. Unlike their earlier grindcore efforts, *Heartwork* is a record that sounds like skilled musicians straining at the edges of their own ability to make something more accomplished.

'We just wanted to push the band and ourselves as hard as possible,' Steer continues. 'We were really playing to the limits of our ability, maybe beyond in places, but we were quite ambitious in a musical sense. We really wanted to do something different that didn't sound like a lot of the music we'd been hearing in the underground.'

Technical ecstasy

With Death and Carcass leading the charge, excitement was building for a more technical kind of death metal. Inspired by the raw musicianship, acts like Atheist and Cynic – both Death spinoffs – took on jazz fusion influences and ran with them, using their involvement with Chuck Schuldiner to propel their projects forward. At the same time, bands like Gorguts and Cryptopsy emerged, with a grimier bent on the technicality, adding elements like piano interludes while retaining an oppressive atmosphere. Now there was a standard for death metal that was more legible and composed than ever, leaning into detailed musicianship as a means to express more complicated emotions and concepts.

'Death metal has its own side pocket of bands that have played around with the limitations of the genre,' opines Cryptic Shift's Ryan Sheperson, a current practitioner of what came to be called 'technical death metal'. 'There's a lot of bands that have come and gone in that time who have tried to push the envelope a little bit – records like Gorguts's *Obscura*, Pestilence's *Spheres*, Cynic's *Focus*, Death's *Human* – the kind of stuff where they've kept some of the traditional foundations of the sound and applied their own style or outside influence.'

Many of the records Sheperson mentions helped shape this era. By this point Atheist had already released their landmark 1991 record, *Unquestionable Presence*, playing a wildly technical style with a heavy focus on the interplay between guitarists.

Then things got weirder. Notable examples include Pestilence's 1993 release, *Spheres*, which found the Dutch outfit experimenting with the jazzy style that Death pioneered on *Human*, adding guitar synth textures and a warm, rich bass sound that snaked around themes of mind control and spiritual energy. Prior to making their landmark album *Obscura* in 1998, Gorguts dropped 1993's *The Erosion of Sanity*, which contrasted dramatic technical elements with acoustic guitar and piano interludes. In 1994, Cryptosy released the sophisticated *Blasphemy Made Flesh*, which married extreme speed with complex and dramatic guitar and bass, using the momentum to elevate their ideas from complex to just plain overwhelming. And in 1996, Edge of Sanity released their landmark record *Crimson*, featuring just one track at 40 minutes, written as a symphony, complete with recurring themes and motifs.

It wasn't just speed or precision that captured their attention. Bands were finding that expanding their songcraft allowed them to explore pathways that had hitherto been unexplored, a notable example being Suffocation's development on 1993's *Breeding the Spawn.*

'We wanted to touch on the bases of the heavy parts, the technicals, the guitar solos, the dark melodies, the upper melodies – making a song have a beginning, a middle, and an end, and a story,' Terrance Hobbs explains of Suffocation's writing philosophy. 'We didn't wanna make something brutally aggressive that was just sterile.'

As label rosters were starting to fill up, scene elders took more risks, opening the floodgates for younger bands to open people's minds to what death metal could be. As new sound avenues opened, there were obvious pressures on death metal musicians to go a little further with their art.

'People are in their garage making a demo, and once they get into a studio they're gonna want to use the [recording equipment],' Keith Kahn-Harris explains. 'It offers all sorts of temptations. Even without trying, you start to become good at your instrument, you're gonna want to do things with it.'

Focus (1993)

Continuing the tradition of Death's ex-members going on to greatness, *Human*-era players Paul Masvidal and Sean Reinert – who had already formed Cynic before joining Death – released *Focus* in 1993. They added twists such as vocals run through a vocoder, which added a strange, alien vibe to the classic death growl. These bands continued to cross-pollinate when early Cynic bassist Tony Choy appeared on Pestilence's 1991 album, *Testimony of the Ancients*, and Atheist's 1993 effort *Elements*.

There are a lot of ways to die in space, and *Focus* is a link to death beyond the stars. Guitars twist together like winding snakes, whilst the robotic voices, shifting the vocals into new territories, confront the audience with horror from beyond our galaxy. What better way to communicate these ideas than perplexing music pushed to the far reaches of human ability, the result of many years dedicated to microscopic improvements. A more technical form of death metal hints at an ability beyond human capabilities, and yet it's wrapped up in very real human anxieties.

Orchid (1995)

In Scandinavia, bands like Opeth were expanding death metal's sound in an entirely different way. Having formed in 1989, lineup frustrations meant they didn't release their first record, *Orchid*, until 1995.

Incorporating elements of British progressive rock, like long melodic passages, intricate and fragile melodies, and acoustic instrumentation, Opeth were yet more proof that death metal could change and adapt by absorbing non-traditional elements that were wildly outside of the usual wheelhouse. This was also an early example of clean singing being featured alongside the death growl, showing the full range of vocalist and guitarist Mikael Åkerfeldt.

Orchid sounds like gentle decay, the cruel passing of time over a delicate stone sculpture. The softer moments are still sinister, but they have a forlorn vibe that their American and British cousins lacked. If this is music that encourages thinking about death, a sudden break allows the listener to be alone with their thoughts, a touch more personally harrowing than a zombie outbreak.

Slaughter of the Soul (1995)

That same year saw the landmark release of *Slaughter of the Soul* from Earache's new signing At the Gates, who formed from the ashes of Grotesque.

'[Grotesque] painted ourselves in a corner, because we could do more of the same but not really take it further,' explains At the Gates frontman Tomas Lindberg.

> It was evil death metal with some black metal burning crosses, and corpse paint. We couldn't do weird stuff, it was really self contained. When we broke up we said that we didn't want to have any boundaries. We looked at bands that inspired us, like Celtic Frost, who did whatever they wanted, and King Crimson, not so much musically, but the attitude. For At the Gates, we wanted to do as much as possible all the time: weird time signatures, different harmonics, minor chords, stuff like that.

Slaughter of the Soul is melodic and weird, cleaner than their brethren in Entombed but dirtier than the blistering technical bands in America. With it, Earache had an instant classic on its hands, and it helped spark a new wave that included fellow Swedish acts like In Flames and Hypocrisy, who released *The Jester Race* and *Abducted* respectively in 1996, using similar melodic techniques. While this music would come to be known loosely as 'melodic death metal', or simply 'melodeath', there was a little pushback on the label, which seems paradoxical in a genre founded on ugly sounds.

'We thought of ourselves as a death metal band,' Lindberg tells me. 'Melodic death metal? I don't really know what that is. Perhaps humans have a need to categorise things in general. My favourite example is grunge, comparing the Melvins to Pearl Jam: they just happen to be underground music that came out at the same time.'

All the same, the term is in common usage now, and it's worth digging into why death metal with melody works. In a similar way to Carcass's *Heartwork*, At the Gates take influence from bands like Iron Maiden and twist the guitar melodies into something darker, shedding the pomp of their stadium-filling forebears.

If the idea of something more tuneful suggests a softening of sentiment, that's not the case in practice. Morbid melodies are all the better for striking a sinister tone and fomenting a bleak atmosphere. It adds sparkle and shine to some revolting ideas, giving shape and pattern to the madness. After all, death is the same outcome, whether by a freak event or the machinations of a considered plot.

Slaughter of the Soul sounds like asphyxiating on a rollercoaster, flooding one's brain with pleasant chemicals as the soul gradually leaves the body. It's discombobulating to associate fun with death. But celebration is not just a valid reaction to dying, it's the heart of what makes death metal compelling. For this reason, and despite what this movement is called, death metal with melody makes all the sense in the world.

Challenging death

The movements towards technicality or melody may have been popular, but plenty of musicians rejected this in favour of a familiar, dirty sound.

A particular example of this was Entombed's hugely influential 1991 debut, *Left Hand Path*, which marked the repulsive and primal chainsaw guitar as a beloved cornerstone of this period. The release of 1993's *Wolverine Blues* saw them change tack to a slower, groovier sound, reminiscent of popular metal act Pantera, a style that is loosely called 'death "n" roll'. But not everyone's trajectory was to get cleaner.

Meanwhile, a familiar sound had spawned a whole scene of its own. Grindcore was virile against the odds, siring several extremely niche microgenres, and taking influences from closely related movements like the punk-metal hybrid 'powerviolence'. There's an enormous amount of crossover with these genre labels and many of them are hotly contested. Nonetheless, a brief overview gives an insight into how many revolting new ideas and directions were emerging.

One such example was the logically named 'deathgrind', which walked the thin line between the musicianship of death metal and the unhinged bombast of grindcore. Exemplified by albums like Assück's *Anticapital* (1991) and Brutal Truth's *Extreme Conditions Demand Extreme Responses* (1992), the style pushed the sound forward but eschewed the overwhelming majority of the melody.

By the mid-1990s, the scene had divided further, and the style known as 'goregrind' developed. Using the gruesome body horror themes of torture and botched operations, they kept the snare sound tight and high-pitched and the vocals inhumanly low, sometimes using pitch-shifting to achieve the desired depth. Stemming from Carcass, this included bands like General Surgery and Regurgitate, who notably releasing the *Necrology* EP (1991) and *Effortless Regurgitation of Bright Red Blood* (1994), respectively. The general vibe is a messier, less distinct form of grindcore with extremely explicit medical details describing failed experiments of the most revoltingly imaginative sort – a kind of John Carpenter on bad shrooms aesthetic.

The will to transgress was taken to sordid extremes in the smut obsessed 'pornogrind', as typified on Gut's 1995 record, *Odour of Torture,* with tales of genital mutilation and frenzied dissections. Outside of this sexually explicit niche, but with similarly offensive intentions, acts like Anal Cunt diverted from socially conscious lyrics to vacillate between scatological humour and the sort of taste-boundary breaking so offensive that it's largely unprintable.

Anal Cunt cross over into noisecore, getting right to the boundary where music breaks down altogether. The best example of this is their outright baffling 1989 offering *5,643 Song EP,* which layers songs over one another to create a confusing, muddled effect. The overlapping effect isn't too far from something Merzbow would dream up.

Grindcore would go on to experimental, technical highs of its own with mathcore bands like Dillinger Escape Plan and Botch both releasing *Calculating Infinity* and *We Are the Romans* in 1999. A year later, Discordance Axis would release *The Inalienable Dreamless*, an immaculately played record with sprightly melodic passages. For now though, it was comfortable acting as a reminder that death is often ignominious, and sometimes a little gross.

Black metal

Influenced by similar sources, from dark thrash bands like Slayer to the thrill of transgressive acts like Venom, the forests of Norway were starting to crackle with a new, bleaker sound that rivalled even the most extreme metal. The harsh blast beats remained, frequently played for more sustained periods, and the terrifying vocals were transposed to a higher pitched howl.

Forged by bands like Mayhem, Burzum and Darkthrone, 'Norwegian black metal' came to prominence in the 1990s. From its birth, the harsher style was deeply mired in controversy. Intent on unleashing the most real and threatening form of metal possible, this tight-knit scene took on a cult-like form, with musicians adopting pseudonyms, painting themselves in corpse paint and using human bones and impaled animal heads in their stage shows. The extreme lifestyle went beyond performance to include acts of true violence and terror. Most famously, Burzum mastermind Varg Vikernes was sent to prison for stabbing his bandmate Øystein 'Euronymous' Aarseth twenty-seven times and burning three churches to the ground.[1] Today he remains engaged in far-right political activities.

'Black metal … that was really scary at one time,' recalls Dave Hunt. 'It might seem silly to say that now, but there was a reality to it.'

Many of these bands had cut their teeth playing death metal, as Darkthrone had with their early records, before switching to a frostier black metal style for 1992's *A Blaze in the Northern Sky*, whilst still signed to heavyweights Peaceville. This was the only band of the style signed to a reputable label – one that was famous for releasing death metal, no less.

Part of the allure of black metal was that it embraced a deathly seriousness that death metal ironically didn't have. A common thread through many of my interviews was that, from behind the Iron Curtain or in the grimy suburbs of

Birmingham, bands were invested in making metal that was escapist, or occasionally tongue-in-cheek. There was a streak of irony to even some of the most lurid descriptions, whereas black metal was utterly dour and joyless.

This presented an existential threat to death metal. These bands were living the lifestyle they were singing about, which made death metal seem less extreme in comparison, damaging any authenticity they'd accrued through the decade. Worse, black metal was openly hostile towards death metal.

'You can't really understand black metal without understanding the context within death metal,' Keith Kahn-Harris explains.

> As much as it was apparently about rebelling against Christianity, it was really about rebelling against Florida: 'Look at these bands wearing white Hi-Tec ankle high boots and blue jeans.' The critique was that you had this thing that was incredibly subversive and challenging, and you domesticated it; you hadn't lived it properly, you've musically tamed it, and that's why Burzum sounds deliberately awful.

This represented a direct challenge to the hegemony of the Morrisound bands. Here was an alternative that didn't just reinterpret their ideas but rejected them outright. It also provided an alternative for metalheads with an increasingly diverse range of options. Black metal's commitment was compelling, and the idea of something darker was certainly refreshing.

'Being deliberately lo-fi requires enormous focus and obsession,' notes Kahn-Harris. 'Producing very dirty lo-fi albums for decades, in the way Darkthrone does, is not an easy thing to do.'

Death in the spotlight

Despite these gathering threats, energies were bubbling up, and larger labels were starting to smell blood.

By the mid-1990s, smaller death metal labels were well established. Earache was leading with bands like Napalm Death, Bolt Thrower and Carcass. Metal Blade's comparative late entry hadn't hampered them, with Cannibal Corpse releasing a string of huge records: 1991's *Butchered at Birth*, 1992's *Tomb of the Mutilated* and 1994's *The Bleeding*. Labels like Peaceville, Roadrunner and Nuclear Blast weren't far behind on signing up the new wave of death metal bands.

'When something breaks musically, it's like a feeding frenzy to make sure that your label had at least one death metal band, or one Bay Area thrash band, or one grunge band,' Ian Glasper comments. 'You needed your token death metal band.'

Major label involvement wasn't wholly alien. Earache already had a distribution deal with Columbia, strengthened by their US label manager Jim Welch moving to act as their director of A&R in 1993.[2] Doing so meant he kept a channel open for Earache bands, and eventually Columbia distributed records including Entombed's *Wolverine Blues* (1993) and Napalm Death's *Fear, Emptiness, Despair* (1994).[3]

In the meantime, Metal Blade was working with Warner, albeit with some caveats. Having previously had kickback over the explicit content of the gross-out theatrical outfit GWAR, they thought it wise to omit their newest and most provocative signing.

'When we signed Cannibal Corpse, they were the only act we didn't put through Warner,' recalls Brian Slagel. 'We thought, "Yeah this might be a bit much for major labels to deal with," so we put them on a separate deal with an independent distributor.'

Despite some teething issues, they were ready to take the risk. With Carcass now in a position to move on, they were stunned to be offered a direct major label deal with the iconic Columbia Records – home to names like Bob Dylan, Miles Davis and Frank Sinatra – in 1993.

'We were completely dazed. It was just crazy to have that thrust upon us, but we were really up for it,' remembers Bill Steer. 'It didn't make a whole lot of sense considering how the band started. We didn't have some kind of long-term plan; it was just tiny little incremental steps. A major label was never on our horizon, ever.'

This was a major opportunity for death metal. A few years prior, no one realistically thought they were going to hit the big time, and the successes were hard-earned. With a crowded scene and challenges coming from nastier forms of music, this momentum was constantly under threat. Naturally, there were some doubters even from the inside.

'Personally for me, I didn't see that whole Columbia thing working out [for Carcass],' says Chris Reifert. 'I just thought, "they're gonna be disappointed."'

Swansong (1996)

Highlighting how much of a gamble this was, Carcass were given a lavish advance to make their fifth record. In a 1996 interview with Rock Hard, bassist Jeff Walker put this at $250,000,[4] comparing favourably to Autopsy's $5,000. But between discovering immediate tension with Columbia and their own interpersonal drama – including the departure of lead guitarist Michael Amott – they found it harder and harder to record.

Hoping for something commercially viable, the label were at odds with the band, who were writing and experimenting with new sounds, and weren't used to dealing with the pressures of a more demanding label.

'I don't have any particular bitterness about how it happened,' Bill Steer says of the ill-fated *Swansong* sessions.

> I just don't think it was meant to be because our band just wasn't structured that way. We didn't have that level of professionalism required, and we certainly weren't gonna cave in to the whims of these characters in New York City ringing us up week after week with different suggestions. You could tell the whole thing was finished very quickly.

Released in 1996, *Swansong* is a curious beast, but certainly not what anyone thought death metal, or Carcass, ought to be. The record is straightforward in places, but flecked with esoteric flourishes that wouldn't be out of place on a Hawkwind album, like the phaser effect on 'Tomorrow Belongs to Nobody', or the strange, lullaby-like structure of 'Black Star'. It retained a little of the morbid Carcass humour on tracks like 'Keep on Rotting in the Free World', but was unfocused and lacked the intensity that attracted fans in the first place.

Unhappy with the results and the unresolved personnel issues, Columbia dropped them before the record could be released. Carcass had the last laugh when they were able to finish the album with the resulting settlement money, and then got paid a second time by re-signing with Earache. The record was released alongside a few remixes, notably one of Björk's song 'Isobel'. But by the time it was out in the wild, and as the album title foretold, they had already split up.

Carcass is the poster child for the clash between major label interest and death metal theatrics, and the failed experiment came at a tipping point for death metal. At the same time, Cannibal Corpse lost vocalist Chris Barnes, Napalm Death lost Barney Greenway and David Vincent left Morbid Angel. Worse, rising stars At the Gates broke up following their breakthrough debut, *Slaughter of the Soul*. Suddenly, as the scene got crowded and money got stretched, many of the smaller bands were being dropped by labels who had snapped up more than they could handle.

Despite a string of blistering records, Roadrunner dropped Gorguts after 1993's *The Erosion of Sanity*. Two years later they dropped Suffocation – today one of the world's premier death metal acts – following 1995's *Pierced from Within*. This fate awaited a whole string of upcoming bands who emerged at the wrong time.

'Growing up you would hear things on TV or radio, like "You need to have a lawyer and you need to go over your music contract,"' recalls Terrance Hobbs. 'Going into the studio we really didn't know how things worked. We didn't know how to record a record. When you realise what Roadrunner did, they had all these heavy bands and one by one they were being dropped. So that was an eye-opening experience.'

The buzz around large scale touring was also coming to an end.

'In '95 we went to the US with Morbid Angel and thought it was gonna be the biggest thing, but you could definitely feel the boom was over,' says Tomas Lindberg. 'Fewer people were interested, and people who had jumped on the bandwagon had disappeared. There was only the underground left, and the venues were probably slightly too big.'

This period marked the end of a major era in death metal. For those paying attention to wider cultural cycles, the genre's mainstream decline was perhaps inevitable after its surprising rise.

It's worth noting that 1994 had seen the death of Nirvana's Kurt Cobain and the sudden end of an extremely influential alternative band. With his loss, the shift in sensibilities that grunge had caused started to slacken, and as the buzz died labels would start to look elsewhere for their next big hit. But it was also the case that labels had taken on too many death metal bands to manage.

'That happened to US hardcore and thrash metal – all those UK thrash bands who signed to majors all got dropped after one record,' observes Ian Glasper.

> Bearing in mind they're on the same roster as Mariah Carey; they're not gonna sell anywhere near that. The other thing is that the A&R guy that signed them – he'll move on and suddenly they're all alone in the label with no friends, and then it's game over for you. And then you've got the stigma attached because you've been dropped by a major label.

'We went through the '80s and lost 20-something bands to major labels,' recalls Brian Slagel of the era prior to death metal.

> None of them succeeded. I don't wanna sit here and say that major labels are terrible because they are not, but a lot of them aren't prepared to deal with stuff that's not in their wheelhouse. So while it's cool for the bands and obviously gives the bands a lot more visibility, a lot of it came back to where it should be: independent labels where they had more freedom to do what they want.

This wasn't the end of the road for death metal, but it was a major turning point for bands. Unlikely though their dreams of mainstream success had always been, there was a slim window where they were achievable, and now they were a distant memory.

What the bursting of the death metal bubble amounted to, though, was a lot of veteran bands who were struggling, and a lot of younger bands who were cut off just as they were developing their style. Without financial backing, it was difficult to progress with just the support of the underground, which many of them hadn't been an active part of for many years.

'We had less contact with it really,' admits Bill Steer.

> I think it's safe to say none of us had been tape trading for a couple years. We were probably reading fewer fanzines and paying less attention to the bands we were playing with. There was a healthy rivalry going on with a lot of those groups: you'd be friends, you'd enjoy playing shows together, but you wouldn't necessarily be listening to each other's albums at home.

With so many bands suddenly gone or cut off at the legs, the landscape looked very different indeed.

'It was a time of dismay for a lot of us aspiring metal folks when we saw our icons wandering off,' says Nile guitarist Karl Sanders. 'Like, "Hey, wait a minute! You're supposed to be our leaders. What are you doing?"'

5 New frontiers (1996–2013)

Jeff and Cyrus, young boys from Texas, form a death metal band. Debating their name and doodling their logo, they practise in Jeff's bedroom. Disturbed by their satanic dalliances, concerned adults separate them, sending Jeff away to a correctional school. Their motivations calcify from hope to spite, but their desire for dark musical mastery is never quelled.

This is the plot to 'The Best Ever Death Metal Band out of Denton', from The Mountain Goats' faultless 2002 indie rock record *All Hail West Texas*. By the late 1990s and early 2000s death metal was a distant cultural memory, a romantic lost cause. Nonetheless, it was still practised.

'Metal in the '90s was pretty much looked at as a dying genre. I remember in 1996 or '97, *Rock Hard* magazine in Germany had a gravestone on the cover,'[1] says Metal Blade's Brian Slagel.

> The underground was great though. Between Cannibal Corpse and Six Feet Under we were selling a lot of records. A couple of bands were selling 100,000 records, which for a death metal band was a lot. And then you start seeing the genre kinda reinvent itself. No major labels, no pressure from mainstream media, you could make the music you wanna make. I think that created the run up to the early 2000s, where death metal and metal in general have this massive resurgence.

While death metal had missed its chance for Learjets and solid gold toilets, the cursed reward was that it could continue being gross and weird in its own little niche. Between the decline in the late 1990s and the turn of the millennium, bands like Obituary, Deicide and Cannibal Corpse continued to tinker with their formulas while putting out strong records such as *Back from the Dead* (1997), *Serpents of the Light* (1997) and *Gallery of Suicide* (1998), respectively. Rising out of Greenville, South Carolina, Nile fused a ferocious, technical style with Egyptian scales. And back in Sweden, Opeth leaned into sombre progressive rock with *Morningrise* (1996) and *My Arms, Your Hearse* (1998), inspiring a healthy underground to make further adjustments to the classic death metal style.

Death metal lost absolutely none of its magic in this period. These albums are every bit as brutish as their predecessors, sometimes moving forward by harkening back to the genre's earlier references, with Nile discussing strange and arcane Lovecraftian deities, and Opeth musing on decay and abandonment.

Having spoken to people who were active in these years, a lot of them were simply staying the course, bemused at a brief run of popularity, and content to drop back into the shadows.

'We didn't have visions of conquering the planet. We just kept going,' says Chris Reifert. 'People are like, 'Oh, death metal died in the mid-to-late '90s. No. You just weren't paying attention. Sometimes you have to poke around and scratch under the surface.'

Filling the void

Whilst the genre was dipping back underground, more distantly influenced bands were starting to rise. 'Industrial metal' took some of the speed and aggression of death metal and fused it with drum machines and harsh mechanical sounds, ending with something distant from even the most distorted human voice.

'I think the earliest sorts of stirrings in that regard would have been Fear Factory,' recalls Bill Steer. 'That sounded extremely modern to our ears. They were introducing different elements that were totally alien to us.'

But when death metal returned to the shadows, it found its old void had been filled by the emerging black metal scene. The darkness and theatricality emanating out of Norway had gripped the hearts and minds of people seeking transgressive music and won a lot of admirers. Now the vests and jeans of death metal seemed inadequate next to corpse paint, black leather, and heavy spikes. Besides, black metal had committed actual murders. How much more transgressive can you get?

'The late '90s was when Emperor, Dimmu Borgir, and Cradle of Filth became the hot new thing,' says *The Punk Rock MBA's* Finn Mckenty. 'I specifically remember that I stopped reading a lot of metal magazines around '96 or '97, because all these magazines like *Pit* and *Metal Maniacs* were starting to write more about black metal than death metal. That was the changing of the guard to me.'

The Norwegian bands who initially railed against the polished sound from Florida would later come to be less hostile to death metal, incorporating it back into their aesthetic to make their permafrost-tinged howls a touch more coherent. Starting with Immortal's 1997 release *Blizzard Beasts,* the fusion style spread further with Behemoth's *Pandemonic Incantations* (1998) to become what is known now as blackened death metal. Later examples such as Belphegor's almighty *Necrodaemon Terrorsathan* (2000) and Akercocke's sexually-charged *Choronzon* (2003) added depth and colour, leaving more traditional death metal acts looking old-fashioned.

Whilst this was happening in the bowels of the underground, a stranger phenomenon came from the wider metal scene. The people who predicted that huge sellers would come from the world of extreme metal weren't entirely wrong when 'nu metal' broke onto the scene. Bands like Slipknot and Korn took an extreme sound, occasionally using the harsh voice, and fused it with a variety of funk, alternative metal and hip-hop sounds.

'Slipknot and Korn did something entirely different,' says Bill Steer. 'It was extremely clever because it resonated with so many people around the world. You can't really say that about the strict death metal bands, who were much more niche.'

Slipknot was absolutely not death metal, lacking the commitment to the guttural vocals, but something adjacent to the genre had truly broken through to the mainstream in a meaningful way. Today they headline festivals alongside Metallica and have sold over 30 million records worldwide.[2]

Sound of Perseverance (1998)

After releasing the complex *Symbolic* (1995), Death unveiled their final entry.

The Sound of Perseverance is the final divide between death metal's older style and the sounds yet to come. Undoubtedly Schuldiner's finest hour, his wild guitar lines explore wide emotional ground, dancing from soaring heights to crushing lows. Richard Christie's dry cymbal hits punctuate glorious instrumental sections on 'Scavenger of Human Sorrow' contrasting with the gloomy bass lead of 'Spirit Crusher'.

With their last breath, Death stared into the face of inner turmoil on 'Bite the Pain', discussed dark sensuality in 'Flesh and the Power it Holds' and worked through the darkness to self-reflect in 'A Moment of Clarity'. The album title is telling; this is death metal in an advanced form, discussing human suffering as an ongoing project, overcoming to dark impulses and self-hatred and coming out the other side.

They caped it off with a riotous cover of Judas Priest's 'Painkiller', where Schuldiner's raspy voice is elevated to high screams. For a band so concerned with the drama of human existence they never lost sight of how much fun they could have, and the fantasy of a robot saviour seems an almost tongue-in-cheek ending to a difficult record.

As the millennium came around, darker times struck. Death stopped work so Chuck Schuldiner could undergo radiotherapy for a brain tumour, before passing away in 2001 at the age of thirty-four. He was remembered fondly by many of the people interviewed for this book.

'I was very fortunate,' says Chris Reifert. 'What I remember the most besides making [*Scream Bloody Gore*] was all the non-band activities: hanging out and watching movies and doing stupid shit, drinking cheap beer and being goofy teenage dorks. It was an innocent time.'

'Chuck was a singular musical talent,' remembers Dave Hunt, who toured with Schuldiner in Benediction, towards the end of his life. 'Metal touring musicians, you can expect them to be like, "Where are the groupies, and where is my peanut butter to cover them in?" He was much more introspective and thoughtful, much more of a role model than if he'd been more extroverted.'

Death's preeminent legacy lives on across the genre. Over the next decade, bands like Obscura, Born of Osiris, Rivers of Nihil and Meshuggah would continue to push the envelope for complex technical music. Later, Schuldiner would be honoured by the Death to All tours, where a rotating line-up of ex-Death members and special guests would perform Death classics.

Blackwater Park (2001)

Death weren't the only band flying the flag for death metal in this period; Opeth had honed their sound, and on their fifth record they married a majestic death metal sound with the delicate aesthetic they'd hinted at their whole career.

Blackwater Park tells tales of failed love, isolation and martyrdom. It takes their flirtation with acoustic sounds to a new level with 'Harvest', a clean-sung waltz which eschews all conventions of death metal. This foreshadowed their eventual total swing away from the genre for 2011's *Heritage,* where they abandoned the death growl to focus on their prog roots.

Attaining critical acclaim far outside its niche *Blackwater Park* is beloved by many who aren't traditional extreme metal fans, once reaching #55 on *Rolling Stone's* '100 Greatest Metal Albums of all time'.[3] To celebrate their landmark achievement, 2010 saw the release of *In Live Concert at the Royal Albert Hall,* where they played the record in full, bringing death metal at one of the world's most prestigious venues.

In Their Darkened Shrines (2002)

In many ways, Nile were a more straightforward death metal project than Opeth or Death, marrying Egyptian scales with the work that their peers had been undertaking but not straying too far from the formula that had made the genre great. But with this release they broke new ground for extreme sounds, proof that death metal still had the capacity to sound rich and sinister.

In Their Darkened Shrines is the sound of being lost in deep catacombs, hunted by unspeakable, unknowable foes. The dark ambient sections in 'Sarcophagous' evoke eerie rituals, contrast with the frantic riffing in much the same way that 'Harvest' does, and they tighten the atmosphere, ready for this to be released when the aggression kicks back in.

For all the outrageous sections and new ideas, Nile were proof that death metal didn't have to stray too far from what made death metal great in the first place. The low intonations in 'Kheftiu Asar Butchiu' and the lightning-fast guitar work of 'The Blessed Dead' built on the foundations of the genre, proof there was still space for the genre to expand within its own boundaries.

Death metal wasn't running out of ideas, but these successes were fewer and further between. Suddenly, it found itself in a humbling world where it could no longer compete financially, and had to watch as the bands it opened the gateways for outstripped it.

'It's an interesting period to touch on the late '90s, early 2000s,' says Dave Hunt, who joined Benediction in 1998.

> We used to laugh and joke in the years that followed that we should have just split up and reformed 10 years later. Carcass, At the Gates, and various other bands did so and came back magnified in their importance, whereas there we were in the period where death metal was licking its wounds, simply too stupid or too stubborn to die. If you look at the explosion at the start and the enduring popularity, that bit in the middle was a bit of a shit time to be a creative.

New technologies

With the breaking of a new millennium, the stage was set for a new legion of younger voices to come out in force. Initially, physical music formats were a little harder to come by.

'I remember there was not a record store that sold death metal or black metal near where I lived [in California],' Carnifex frontman Scott Ian Lewis recalls. 'I had to drive to Oceanside where there was a store which was half a record store and half a sex shop. That was the only place you could find extreme metal! It was like a hippie shop, and then some secret metalhead worked there.'

However, this scarcity was changing rapidly. After once again dipping into the safe but harder-to-access underground, new technologies would unlock death metal for a new generation. New avenues were opening for distribution as dedicated labels made things a lot easier for fans, who could order records directly or go to a record store. Then things really changed when traditional physical media began melting away in the face of the digital revolution.

'I remember the early days of the internet,' says Dave Hunt. 'I found it so intoxicatingly special that I could find something on there that was talking about a band called The Abyss, which was a black metal offshoot of Hypocrisy. You still had a feeling that people didn't know about this. There was something transgressive where your name might be on a surveillance list because you've even looked at it.'

With the growing availability of the internet, death metal's underground channels were cheaper, faster and easier to access. It was no longer necessary to painstakingly mail cassettes out, but, as Hunt describes, there was still a darkness to swapping music through shoddy, homemade websites while attempting to negotiate a minefield of viruses.

While the inevitable demise of physical album sales seriously hurt an artist's ability to monetize their music, it opened a new generation of fans who could freely share music, through either burned CDs or, more powerfully, MP3 files that could be sent via email and messaging services, uploaded to blogs and streamed on burgeoning social media sites such as Myspace. Tech-savvy fans could download every album ever known to man from torrenting sites like Limewire, Napster or Kazaa, and cheerfully fry their hard drives whilst streaming all of Behemoth's discography.

For the younger generation, music blogs also replaced fanzines and record store clerks as the arbiters of taste and discovery.

'I think the major difference between [the internet] and tape trading is speed,' says Keith Kahn-Harris. 'Things happen much more rapidly now; the barriers to entry are much less; the degree of commitment is much less. What's the same is the desire to find rarity – the delight in obscurity.'

With technological changes allowing listeners to go deeper without the barriers of money or time, new artists seized the opportunity with both hands. By the early 2000s, the same undercurrents of extreme music that had united people in Stockholm and Birmingham were drawing people together in new, often virtual places, and with new influences. Just as Ian Glasper described a melting pot of ingredients that forged early grindcore, new ideas were bubbling up from unexpected quarters, and older barriers were starting to be brought down as kids had rapid access to new music. Adjusting to this new internet age, death metal was changing fast.

Rotten to the core

Buoyed by the success of Slipknot and Korn, the mainstream had a number of newer bands who were grabbing the baton passed on by death metal.

'Around the same time as the rise of deathcore is when Killswitch Engage and Lamb of God started coming up as well,' Finn Mckenty remembers. 'So there were a couple of sea changes between the downfall of the Earache and Roadrunner death metal scene and the rise of deathcore.'

Grouped into the 'New Wave of American Heavy Metal', successful bands like Lamb of God, Trivium and Shadows Fall were aligned closer to extreme metal than the groups who found wild success at the end of the 1990s. For kids growing up then, it wasn't a big jump to get into something even heavier or more obscure.

'When I was a teenager in the early 2000s, I was getting into heavier music like the mix of hardcore, death metal, and metalcore,' Scott Ian Lewis recalls. 'A lot of the bands were referencing [At the Gates] – *Slaughter of the Soul* was one of the first old-school death metal records that I really got into. And Darkest Hour, they were really heavy on that sound. The Black Dahlia Murder's first record, *Unhallowed* – I'd seen their video on [MTV's] *Headbanger's Ball* – I kinda dove deep into it.'

What emerged came to be known as 'deathcore', whose name came from 'metalcore': a heavy fusion of metal and hardcore that stripped some of the more indulgent elements of metal, like extended guitar solos, and replaced them with breakdowns, slower sections that lean into a weighty groove. The vocals were expanded with singers switching between gruff growl or screams and clean singing.

'In '05, metalcore was crazy popular,' Lewis tells me.

We were like, OK, metalcore is cool, but what if you cut off all the singing shit and you just play the heavy shit and breakdowns? What if your drummer is a death metal drummer? And what if your vocalist is more influenced by Corpsegrinder than he is by [As I Lay Dying's] Tim Lambesis? That's kinda how it came to be.

Pioneering deathcore bands included California's Suicide Silence and Carnifex, and Arizona's Job for a Cowboy. And just as their death metal forefathers had done, they were putting in the work and the hours on the road to get their projects off the ground.

'A lot of the shows we played were local hardcore shows mixing with death metal, which is something you don't see much of these days,' says Job for a Cowboy frontman Jonny Davy. 'Just a mixing of genres and communities. We were so young, an average age of 15, playing in our parents' garages, playing as many local shows as we could. We would drive out to Texas, California, 6 to 8 hour drives, just so we could get out as much as we could.'

'I remember playing a backyard show with the guys in Suicide Silence in 2006,' Lewis recalls of Carnifex's early days. 'It was like 30 kids on a patio in a backyard, moshing on dirt. That was the start of the scene.'

And as if history was repeating itself, they faced many of the same roadblocks their forbearers had.

'Finally we saved some money to record an EP,' Davy recalls. 'We didn't know what we were doing with that. We didn't play to a click track, we just kinda went in there and we slapped it all together with tape and glue, and released it. Even with *Genesis* we were still trying to get our bearings straight and figure out what we wanted to do with the band.'

Genesis (2007)

Released in 2007, Job for a Cowboy's first full-length, *Genesis*, became the highest-selling extreme metal debut since Slipknot's self-titled record. For a genre that had conceded to bands like that many years prior, this was no small feat.

Genesis is the soundtrack to being ripped apart by multiple hands, alternating between blunt blows and scalpel incisions. It's an amalgamation of many forms of death, a freshly horrible experience.

Devastatingly fast and dexterous, *Genesis* is the soundtrack to being ripped apart by multiple hands, alternating between blunt blows and scalpel incisions. It's an amalgamation of many forms of death, a freshly horrible experience. It has technical elements without feeling mechanical, and it rejects clean singing for a ferocious growl. It sounds at one time completely embedded inside death metal, and also somewhat alien.

This was clearly not being made by veterans with a lifetime of making this sort of music, but rather by people approaching it from a separate time and location. Indeed, it was made by kids who were approaching extreme metal holistically, with a wider exposure to a palette encompassing more than traditional death metal alone.

Dead in My Arms (2007)

With multiple bands reaching for the same sound, the new deathcore style was quickly established. Carnifex's debut *Dead in My Arms* dropped in May of the same year, and featured many of the same hallmarks as Job for a Cowboy, skipping between guitar mastery and pummelling percussion.

Notably, the record changed up the traditional death growl. Now it switched between a blistering guttural and higher-pitched scream, with a similar timbre to a metalcore shriek. Just as the death growl was a corruption of the singing voice, this twisted the metalcore standard, where clean and harsh vocals would contrast, into full darkness mode.

Deathcore was embracing new options, and breaking traditions down in order to make them more impactful. It was working. *Dead in My Arms* sounds like a wail of fury at finding a loved one's corpse. Wreathed in melodrama, it's a howl of contorted emotions, grounded in the real, and a far cry from zombie rituals, but no less devastating.

The Cleansing (2007)

Two decades after the explosion of death metal, Suicide Silence's debut capped off a productive year for deathcore while summarizing the many years of refinement and sonic devastation by their predecessors. Cementing the sound and vibe, *The Cleansing* is a relentless record that sounds like getting beaten up whilst soaking in bleach.

The guitars are ferocious, contrasting the low end with the wail of pinch harmonics, that snake around the rapid-fire drums, while the dynamic focal point is vocalist Mitch Lucker, who alternates his growling to include a harrowing shriek. The resultant record is diverse, energetic and stunningly heavy.

The video for 'Price of Beauty', which depicts a plastic surgery disaster, even won Suicide Silence some metal credit for being banned from *Headbanger's Ball*.[4] Despite the lack of support, the record launched the band, positioning them as frontrunners for the movement.

Strengthening the core

By 2008 deathcore had taken on a life of its own, coinciding with the rapid rise of Myspace and other networking tools that helped bands launch their project and nurture their audience. Not only was it easier to share and experience new music, making meaningful and useful connections had been streamlined.

'Myspace had a thing where you could place your 8 best friends on your homepage, so the bands would do that,' Jonny Davy explains. 'We became really good friends with bands like Animosity and Cattle Decapitation back then. I remember that little way to show the masses recommendations. I think that's one of the biggest things that helped us to get as many eyes on us as possible.'

The communities that bands and fans were forming meant they had a readymade audience, just as earlier bands had harnessed through the tape trading scene. It meant that when the time came, records like *Genesis* sold – or were illegally downloaded – like crazy, and bands who were putting the time in to embrace those platforms and tour heavily were rewarded. Soon, the 'deathcore' category was established, even if the genre itself was becoming less defined.

'All of a sudden, in 2008, the term "deathcore" hit real hard because of Myspace,' recalls Scott Ian Lewis. 'The fact that it cemented itself as a genre when we were growing was like, "OK that's cool, but we're not defined by that." If you look at the timeline, it came after our inception; it was never a roadmap we really looked at to begin with.'

In a similar fashion to their grindcore ancestors, cultural barriers melted away as kids with earnest interests in various heavy sounds melded ideas together. A common thread in everyone I spoke to from this era was that they were earnestly trying to be as ruthlessly heavy as possible, taking elements from everything they liked and pushing them as hard as they could, just as bands a decade ago, and a decade before that, had done.

In comparison to other bands from the time – say Mastodon, Trivium or Killswitch Engage – deathcore was focused on weight and volume. The early Job for a Cowboy and Carnifex records sound unhinged, more frantic than their peers. And though the records are rough in some places, as records written by younger bands often are, it was clear that death metal had turned a page. A notable step up in production from a decade ago was aided by new home recording technology like Pro Tools, which made it cheaper and easier for young bands to record and release their own music.

Despite the aesthetic changes, deathcore bands were singing about the same things: railing against religion in Job for a Cowboy's *Reduced to Mere Filth*, mental turmoil in Carnifex's *The Diseased and the Poisoned* and body horror in Suicide Silence's *Eyes Sewn Shut*. It was just as gross as death metal had been a few decades ago, reacting to exactly the same existential pressures as their forebears, but supercharged for a new generation.

Backlash

In what was becoming a time-honoured cycle, deathcore was causing a ruckus, selling records and touring the latest strain of gruesome music around the world. But, just as these bands were rising, an older set of voices were challenging these newcomers.

Whilst kids were eating this up, the old guard saw it as a further death blow. The established traditions were being tinkered with, old rules were being broken, and, having already lost out to Slipknot, it was now seeing its ideas taken and warped by a younger generation that was reaping the financial benefits.

'We had a lot of negative reactions. I think when you get so much attention so fast there's gonna be some backlash,' recalls Davy. 'That was strange for us, especially being so young, but in the end there was nothing we could really do. All those comments, especially in the underground elitist death metal world, gave us a chip on our shoulder. It kinda helped our success and drove us to go more full-out.'

Helping shape this narrative was the metal press who, having seen rapid changes and frustrated that the stalwarts had retreated to the underground, were sceptical of the new sound, despite the fact that it was blisteringly heavy in all the same ways that their champions were. This has often been a sticking point for the genre, and a little bemusing for anyone looking back on this era.

'Deathcore was sonically not very different to death metal, unless you're just the most pedantic, hair-splitting nerd,' says Finn McKenty, who ran the popular blog *Stuff U Will Hate*, which poked fun at old-school death metal fans uncomfortable at the changes in the scene. 'The aesthetic, the scene, and the people who were into it were very different.'

'It was made by kids – in some cases, high school kids,' says Ben Umanov, co-founder and joint editor-in-chief of *Metalsucks*, which shaped many of these attitudes.

I remember Job for a Cowboy specifically got big on Myspace, which at least in its early days was very much a youth-oriented platform. All those bands were influenced by nu metal, so automatically they had a strike against them. If you look back, we're there as 25-year-olds pooh-poohing the stuff that the 18, 19 and 20-year-olds were making at the time. It took a while for us to get over ourselves and realise that some of these bands were making legitimate music.

'Historically, metal fans are always down on whatever's new, at least for a little while,' says fellow *Metalsucks* joint editor-in-chief and co-founder Matt Goldberg.

For its reputation as a free-thinking genre, people are very stuck in their ways. Talk to Mark Heylmun, the guitar player from Suicide Silence. He's like, 'Yeah, the other dudes in the band, we were into Korn'. By any other standard Korn would be considered heavy, but to death metal bands, the fact that we even said Korn is offensive to them.

It's perhaps only natural that the old guard was so upset at all this. Deathcore sounds just different enough to be separate from death metal, made by people who look different. The younger bands were less obviously blue collar dudes, and would experiment with skinny jeans and tighter-fitting shirts, a clear break from the grimy shorts and loose-fitting attire from the past. Shoulder-length hair was no longer a staple, and the breakdowns and alterations to the voice were clear deviations from the norm.

It seems ironic that a genre so obsessed with death would be uneasy at future generations celebrating the great void. For all the threats to its popularity and finances, death metal was now being confronted by its age, a reminder that its own time on earth was limited. Railing against this was a legitimate response to such a fear, but so was deathcore's gradual acceptance into the death metal canon.

Slam it down

As deathcore became gradually more popular, other notable sub-scenes emerged in the underground concurrently.

Characterized by deeper gutturals, slower riffing and a high-pitched, ringy snare, slam was first spewed in the early 1990s. Taking the breakdowns and technical mastery of early Suffocation, especially their 1991 debut, *Effigy of the Forgotten*, bands like Pyrexia ran with the more basic ideas to create the driving bass sound of 1993's *Sermon of Mockery*. Slam shares some of the bounce and groove of nu-metal, and walks back some of the experimentation of earlier death metal, cutting back some of the excesses.

'The band that coined the term "slam" was definitely Internal Bleeding back in '92,' says Finn Mckenty. 'Slam as a genre came into existence around the same time as deathcore, but it was definitely not part of the deathcore scene.'

By the mid-2000s, the scene had its own niche in the underground, with the release of Cephalotripsy's *Uterovaginal Insertion of Extirpated Anomalies* (2007), and Devourment's *Unleash the Carnivore* (2009). Like deathcore, it found rejection from metal tastemakers.

'Slam was shunned and hated by death metal people,' McKenty adds. 'The sonic elements are a subset of death metal, but culturally it's pretty different. Slam has never taken itself seriously, which I think is interesting given that it's so extreme sonically, but the bands themselves are very chilled, lighthearted and self aware.'

Just as grindcore was thriving in the underground during the rise of death metal, slam is a gruesome version of what death metal could be, a tongue-in-cheek answer to the melodrama of deathcore. And whilst it didn't challenge deathcore's growing popularity in the 2000s, it was a reminder that the underground was constantly bristling with new ideas.

Saturation point

As history could have foreseen, deathcore's rapid growth couldn't be sustained forever. By the beginning of the 2010s the genre had swollen drastically, homogenizing the sound.

'There was such a long period of time where it was so saturated,' says Jonny Davy. 'A large percentage of those bands sounded the same, regurgitating the same sounds and ideas. I think that's a big chunk of the negative connotations the deathcore tag had back then.'

As deathcore became a safe bet, the bands had the same issues with labels, which predictably snapped up the emerging groups. Quickly, this led to rough deals for the often very young bands building a name for themselves.

'Winds of Plague came right around the same time as us. Whitechapel signed to Metal Blade. Suicide Silence were on Century Media. Job for a Cowboy and All Shall Perish were on Nuclear Blast from the beginning,' remembers Scott Ian Lewis. 'So I guess every label was like, "Well, we'll sign one."'

But just as death metal acts before them had experienced, many of these bands faced diminishing sales returns, or simply disbanded. Job for a Cowboy's second record, *Ruination* (2009), sold 10,600 copies in its first week,[5] and their third, 2012's *Demonocracy*, sold 4,900.[6] Many of them were dropped or faced label issues, such as Carnifex, who, following disputes with Victory, had a brief hiatus in 2012 and 2013, before emerging on Nuclear Blast.

Deathcore faced another blow when Suicide Silence vocalist Mitch Lucker died in a motorcycle crash in 2012. Following a year of inactivity, they re-emerged in 2013 with new vocalist Eddie Hermida of fellow act All Shall Perish. In a similar vein to the Death to All shows, they organized the *Ending Is the Beginning* live tribute show, with vocalists such as Jonny Davy, Whitechapel's Phil Bozeman and Soulfly's frontman (ex-Sepultura) Max Cavelera filling in.

Deathcore's story does not have a solid ending. Job for a Cowboy are working on new material as I write, and everyone I spoke to was glowing with modern deathcore recommendations.

'I feel like we're on the cusp of a [deathcore] resurgence. You have Lorna Shore, Burn the Sacrifice, Slaughter to Prevail … these are young new bands who are getting embraced from the get-go,' Lewis tells me excitedly. 'They didn't have to lose a few men on the frontlines. We were fighting the industry, fighting critics, now everyone knows you can get on Spotify and you're good to go. Bands can be found very easily now, and fans are embracing what they like. I think deathcore is gonna get the attention it's always deserved.'

'I think the genre has tree-branched into so many genres,' Davy states. 'I just love to see the ideas, the incorporation of other genres, and just trying new things. Obviously I love the traditional stuff – whenever Cannibal Corpse puts out a record I'm always very excited. That's my favourite part of this genre: it keeps expanding and evolving.'

As deathcore came of age, it entered the pantheon of established death metal styles, a further mutation of the rough punk elements. And as a new digital underground grew up around it, it showed that aspiring musicians who wanted to make ugly music had an outlet that wasn't too far from the intensity, the drama and the omnipresent, baleful vocals of the original elixir.

6 Death in the present (2013–21)

A new decade has dawned, and an American teenage girl is vexed. Neither she nor her boyfriend can find her electronic cigarette. As they search, her indignation grows to the point where her soft Valley Girl accent hardens into an animal howl, before brandishing a firearm and rampaging through her suburban neighbourhood. Only when the device is found does her voice revert to its original, innocent form.

This is the plot to 'Where's My Juul??', a 2020 song and viral video by rapper Lil Mariko and producer Full Tac. It's a little bit of a stretch to claim that this is a death metal song. But that horrifying warping of her voice is used to communicate the depth of darkness that only comes from an unpleasant nicotine craving. As she says in a 2020 interview with *Vice*, 'There's more than one way to scream.'[1]

Lil Mariko is right. Death metal's rapid growth in the 1990s and expansion through the 2000s has led to an increasing fractionalization, making it increasingly difficult to track the trends of ideas, moods and sensibilities. The genre's influence today, however murky, shows up in a lot of unexpected places, and through all of extreme metal.

To illustrate this, I spoke with Dave Hunt, whose main project, Anaal Nathrakh, plays a mortifying concoction of black metal, grindcore and harsh electronic noise.

'Death metal has permeated into the wallpaper of the music world,' says Hunt. 'It's undeniably an influence on us, even if it's not a direct one, because it's part of that sound world in general. It's become, in its own way, a sort of mainstream; it was a background against which everything else happened.'

Like many extreme metal bands today, Anaal Nathrakh treats death metal more as a flavour than a dogma. Not only are they talking about death very directly in tracks like 'We Will Fucking Kill You', but their sound is bafflingly horrible, as much from Hunt's baleful growl as it is from the bloodythirsty guitars and electronics.

The extreme metal underground of the dawning 2020s bristles with bands as diverse as Portal, Inter Arma and Ulcerate, all of whom engage with death metal on some level. The aim with this type of music is to compete for the most harrowing sound ever made, and to do so these acts creatively employ classic death metal tropes in new and abstract ways. Elsewhere, mainstream metal bands like Behemoth and Gojira clearly engage with death metal allusions, the former writing complex and bombastic anti-theology and the latter crafting dry, crisp epics about ecological disaster. On the outer reaches of the metal kingdom, you can look to Ghostemane's throat-scouring 2020 track 'Hydrochloride' or the blast beats and howling of Death Grips's 'Giving Bad People Good Ideas' (2016) to see its wide impact.

Although bands like Napalm Death are still making challenging, worthwhile music, it no longer represents the vanguard of transgressiveness. Under the wide umbrella of extreme music, that title more rightfully belongs to artists like Sunn O))), who weaponize volume via a bewildering array of amps, Author & Punisher, an engineer who builds his own destructive music machines to make a metal-flavoured creation transcending genre, or Primitive Man, who blend noise music, hardcore aggression and metal's worship of loudness to formless and devastating effect.

All these artists share some elements with the more experimental side of death metal: the formlessness, the raw aggression, the boundary-pushing speed and ferocity. Aesthetically, however, they have moved away from some of the strict trappings of the genre, even while using the death growl.

Navel-gazing about the slithers of death metal in various extreme metal subsets is a Sisyphean task, and impossible to quantify in a scientific sense. In its fourth decade of influence, death metal isn't a tight mix of genre conventions, it's a vibe, an aesthetic, and one that has been tempered by lots of very talented and imaginative people.

Because death metal is flying off in all directions, it's harder to trace movements. Micro-scenes crop up and wither away, and death metal influence turns up everywhere. The streaming service Bandcamp lists a number of articles digging deep into micro-scenes such as dissonant death metal[2] or German tech-death.[3] Zooming out a little bit, some of the seminal records from the past few years have shaped modern death metal, leading up the pandemic years.

Animus (2016)

Hailing from Wales, Venom Prison's tight, modern sound is slick, polished and mercilessly precise, all while employing chaotic elements from the past. On their 2016 debut, *Animus*, they eschew some of the more rigid song structures in favour of something more gleefully spirited. Here we see elements of the early grindcore bands reimagined as a tight death metal aesthetic; the chaos, the anger and the formless noise clash against one another – but their playing style is deeply accomplished with the grit of grindcore and the magic of technical metal.

'I don't really think we're much different from bands before us,' says vocalist Larissa Stupar, 'but I do think we're keeping the genre alive by bringing in elements from our backgrounds as people in hardcore. For me personally there weren't many metal shows, so hardcore and punk shows were where I got to enjoy live music.'

For people who bemoan that death metal so often takes a non-political stance while so often tolerating violence against women, *Animus* is a breath of fresh air.

'I wanna make people feel uncomfortable,' Stupar tells me. 'I like to remind people these things are real: rape culture is real, sexism is real, racism is real, fascism is real. People suffer every day from the hands of these things and I'd like to open some eyes. That's my number one priority.'

Venom Prison's approach challenges subjects that are generally covered less by death metal, moving back from existential issues and into real-life problems. For anyone watching the world unfurl, this feels timely.

Animus is the sound of a litany of sins being read to you before execution, the knowledge that you thoroughly deserve your punishment. For established death metal fans who may have let misogynist imagery slide in the past, they're an especially galling listen.

Hidden History of the Human Race (2019)

Venom Prison looks to the here and now. But there's a whole universe of suffering to be reckoned with, as shown on two vital releases from the past few years.

Unleashed by Denver, Colorado's Blood Incantation, *Hidden History of the Human Race*, takes the technical metal of bands like Death and Atheist to new places. Sprawling guitars perform superhuman feats, seemingly far beyond the capabilities of humankind. Paul Riedl's vocals, telling of clandestine alien visits, are strange rambles, delivered quite differently to genre standards like Corpsegrinder. The psychedelic effect is surreal and, fittingly, wholly alien.

The familiar trappings of death metal are evident but everything is warped slightly; the blast beats are more fluid and, with a heavy hand on the ride and softer on the snare, they sound jazzier. The guitars don't play riffs as such but cycle through bizarre and complex patterns of notes. Going against the grain of their forebearers, their playing is slacker and decidedly analogue. As a result, they sound more human and more alien simultaneously.

The record cascades over itself, presenting a clash of rhythms, ideas and textures. The record is physical, and despite the athletic feats of the musicians it's possible to imagine this being played by people, unlike using synthesizers or studio magic to evoke a weird or unsettling tone. Plenty of bands have added jazz elements to the death metal style but few have repackaged the expectation of laser precision into something fluid and washy.

Hidden History shows space as unknowable, the soundtrack to humanity making it out beyond the stars and finding that the vastness is maddeningly unwelcome. This is the soundtrack to uncovering dark secrets of our own planet, far beyond the wildest nightmares of H.P. Lovecraft.

Visitations from Enceladus (2020)

While there are a few bands who could play with Blood Incantation's stunning technicality, there are similar acts who are looking to the stars, reaching the same conclusion through different means.

Cryptic Shift play extended tracks, taking the violence of the genre and adding psychedelic washes and wild harmonic bursts to create something jagged and alien. On 2020's *Visitations from Enceladus* they open with a 26-minute song, 'Moonbelt Immolator', which features acid-tinged washes of noise and sudden vocal stabs. The effect is disorientating, stylistically rubbing shoulders with greats like Morbid Angel, but with the song structure and aesthetic of 1970s prog rock.

'I think the way that the songs are written is somewhat unique,' says Cryptic Shift drummer Ryan Sheperson.

> The way that Xander [Bradley, vocals] has written it is like watching a film. The themes in the music are reflective in the lyrics, and it's all based on the emotions and environments, the concepts and stories. I think it gives a lot more substance to the music itself. It's not just the traditional death metal, it's not trying to be an homage to the old school stuff, or keep in line with what's currently coming out.

This is a more extreme version of a melting pot than we've seen previously. Bands who would previously not be seen as such direct influences, like Yes or Camel, are here used as openly as Autopsy or Death. Unlike with Opeth, the delicate sounds are shelved in favour of blinding intensity. In doing so, Cryptic Shift has tapped into something refreshingly transgressive. Not only is it exploratory and conceptual in the same way that prog was, but they're introducing new sounds to the genre – sometimes extremely unpleasant ones like the atonal harmonic stabs in 'Moonbelt Immolator'.

Visitations is the soundtrack to asphyxiation, crash-landings and starvation in the cosmic void. If bands like Blood Incantation represent space as unfathomable, Cryptic Shift's stories tell of a stellar journey filled with materially bleak prospects. Gazing at the universe and dreaming of a prosperous life is the spark that ignites so much science fiction, but there's a lot of death waiting beyond the stars too.

Technical ecstasy

Cryptic Shift and Blood Incantation represent a new breed that takes technical death metal to brave new places. The long tradition of getting increasingly intricate has long been a driving force behind the genre. Sonically, not too much has changed, though the boundaries are continually pushed. Culturally, this scene is clearly distinct from the main body of death metal, which Obscura vocalist and guitarist Steffen Kummerer helped to illustrate.

'It's not only the music, it's the aesthetic,' he tells me. 'Nowadays wearing black long-sleeves, having a fretless bass, playing a thousand notes, sweeping guitar leads, singing about the universe and cosmos – that makes it tech death.'

This aesthetic links them with earlier bands like The Faceless, Rivers of Nihil and Gorguts. It's confrontational in that it is deeply weird, bewildering for even a hardened listener. Records like *Hidden History* can still shock an established audience, and there's much more room for future bands to make it even weirder. To take it back a little, the Morrisound bands who sought a tighter sound, forged in the furnace of Florida, have found their work expanded on many times here.

'Cryptic Shift and Blood Incantation – they sound like they digest everything from the late '80s and early '90s, like old Morbid Angel, Nocturnus,' Kummerer remarks. 'They all have a very broad palette of sounds but they still sound super brutal. They still sound super organic, and not overproduced like a computer game.'

There are further examples of technical death metal expanding further. Meshuggah, who came from death metal to pioneer a mind-expanding version of technical metal, took the ideas expressed by these bands and extended them further, playing with polyrhythms and extended-range instruments to make tense music that feels like a futile attempt to understand the nature of the cosmos with our feeble human minds. Their efforts have expanded into a sprawling array of modern technical metal bands sometimes grouped under the 'djent' group, including Animals as Leaders, Tesseract and Sikth.

An Unexpected Reality (2021)

An Unexpected Reality sounds like an uncomplicated death, like being beaten or stabbed and then left slowly to bleed out. With an unexpected intensity and clarity, it's a death you've endured before, but never in such detail.

The past few examples have shown a genre looking forward, to confront its own demons, or to ponder the future of humanity. *So what about bands looking backwards?*

At first glance, it's tempting to say that old-school death metal bands like Gatecreeper, Tomb Mold, Bloodbath and Gruesome aren't adding anything new. Their approach is a pastiche of death metal, particularly on a record like Gruesome's *Twisted Prayers*, which is practically dripping with the influence of *Scream Bloody Gore*-era Death. These are valid criticisms, although they still work as death metal albums – zombies are still scary.

The new guard is bringing fresh energy to the proceedings, even when the opposite might seem true. An excellent example is Arizona outfit Gatecreeper, who take a thoroughbred stance on how their music should be played and recorded. Their artwork is grisly and raw, and the music could have been plucked from any time in the early 1990s. This also extends to issuing classic long sleeve T-shirts modelled after the cherished death metal art of old.

'I think there are certain things that are traditional that I would like to continue to do,' says vocalist Chase Mason.

> Some of it is aesthetic; I think death metal records should have a cool painting for the cover, like the classic Dan Seagrave art. That's just what a death metal record should have for me. A lot of our band is very referential; it's very influences-on-our-sleeve. We've always put together a Frankenstein's monster of all our different influences. If you took all the stuff we're referencing and split them apart, each one is not very original by any means, but I think together as a whole we are creating something new.

Despite Gatecreeper's traditionalist approach, they continue to reimagine them in exciting new ways. Their 2021 EP, *An*

Unexpected Reality, melds outside elements like doom and grindcore to produce something that is undeniably death metal. To make clear how they identify themselves, their presentation contains all the accoutrements of death metal, such as the classic logo script and the grim artwork of their predecessors.

Emulating an older style is not an issue that's specific to death metal, of course, and it's been done to varying degrees of success, but it's an ongoing feature of the genre. Many of these features lead to new developments later on. Here, bands like Gatecreeper put their stamp on the classic sound, distilling and reconfiguring the elements that work to their benefit.

The Nightmare of Being (2021)

Nightmare is the sound of death catching up with you, having lived with the fear of it for years. Confronting these themes is a slow killer, accepting the darkness over a long period. It's a darker and more considered death, older and nuanced, like being overcome by something you've lived in fear of for many years.

I cannot tell you the number of bands I have watched over the years who have tried to copy At the Gates note for note. For younger fans, it's entirely possible that they've come across a whole host of these bands before encountering *Slaughter of the Soul*. And yet, At the Gates are still making new music. Dropped whilst this book was being written, their seventh record, *The Nightmare of Being,* is a searching and vital creative high point.

The syrup-sweet melodies are still present, twining around Tomas Lindberg's voice, now gruffer with age. Songs are expanded with softer sections, such as the intro to the title track, and dip into saxophone instrumentation on 'Garden of Cyrus'. This is all underpinned by Lindberg's relentless pessimism, lurching from hopelessness on 'The Paradox' to dwindling faith in religious institutions on 'Touched by the White Hands of Death'.

The power of nostalgia is hugely important to death metal, and a new At the Gates record in 2021 is a link to a simpler time when the future of the movement was unwritten. Bands are still using spiky logos, seeking out old pedals to make the same sounds, and training for years to play with the same intensity. There's a huge underground trading scene for vintage death metal merch, and plenty of new bands that are trying to capture the essence of what death metal bands tapped into in the 1990s.

'Metal is a very nostalgic genre in general, and death metal even more so,' Lindberg tells me. 'There are lots of new, young retro bands. Some of them are really good, but I'm old so I would always say, "Why listen to a band who sounds like Repulsion when you could listen to Repulsion?"'

This approach shows an older band adjusting their approach, updating and refining their old ideas just as Carcass, Napalm Death and Cannibal Corpse have. Our understanding of death changes every day, after all.

Future perfect

Joan of Shark, a 1.6 tonne great white, is roused from her slumber by a thunderous sound that shudders through the ocean. Her curiosity aroused, she heads to the source, only to find two other gargantuan creatures circling the boat. Idling, it is blasting ungodly noise as the tiny figures on deck hastily arrange filming equipment. She backs off, leaving the other two to investigate.

So goes the story of the crew filming for the Discovery Channel show *Bride of Jaws*, who attract sharks using death metal played through military-grade underwater speakers, which reportedly mimics the vibrations of struggling fish.[4] This is welcome proof that, aside from easing existential panic, death metal does have some practical use.

Death metal continues to crop up in odd places. In 2020, *Doom Eternal* was released, which features composer Mick Gordon's forty-piece vocal choir of metal singers from across the world, including Sven de Caluwé of Aborted and James Dorton (Black Crown Initiate), to lend a demonic feel to the music.[5] Death metal is no stranger to video games, appearing prominently in titles such as 2009's *Brütal Legend*[6] and sparingly in 2009's *Guitar Hero: Warriors of Rock,* which featured tracks from Dethklok and Children of Bodom.[7] Where Guitar Hero emulates the feeling of playing on stage, the other examples allow a protagonist to create a great deal of death, slaying horrible demons or fantasy creatures, acting out a digital version of the songs. Whether simply part of the soundtrack or woven into the DNA, death metal's impact on gaming has led to new creative avenues, and new places for their music to be heard.

These appearances follow a tradition of death metal garnering unlikely mainstream attention. In the world of wrestling, already no stranger to heavy metal, Australian wrestler Ladybeard moonlights as a death metal vocalist,[8] and two-time world heavyweight champion Jerry Lynn, avowed Dying Fetus fan, would cap off interviews with a heartfelt death growl.[9] In sport, professional footballer and manager of Torino F.C. Ivan Jurić uses his love of Obituary to inspire a high-energy approach to overwhelm his opponents.[10] In politics, Danica Roem, Virginia House of Delegates member and first openly transgender person to be elected to a state legislature, was the vocalist for Cab Ride Home, whose sound falls between thrash and melodic death metal.[11] Elsewhere, French high-fashion company Vetements released a line in 2016 with designs inspired by classic death metal logos and artwork – with pieces priced in excess of $1,000 – a little taste of the forbidden for a sizeable price tag.[12] The genre and aesthetic has been around long enough that these odd meetings are somewhat inevitable, fascinating to creative who crave authentic darkness, and giving musicians the hope that their music might be unexpectedly played to a wider audience, just as Napalm Death enjoyed with Ed Miliband.

In trying to survey the death metal landscape today, I asked some peers for recommendations, and was thrilled at the strange and wonderful bands I got back. There's Slugdge, a slug-themed outfit with titles like 'Salt Thrower', who are as silly as they are accomplished. There's Portal's *Ion* (2018), flying the flag for death metal's avant-garde front, confusing and maddening and difficult beyond belief. There's Ulcerate, who dance between caveman riffs and technical ecstasy, embracing the void between shape and chaos. Their 2020 release *Stare into Death and Be Still* released to huge acclaim, a shining example of death metal embracing a new decade. There's Imperial Triumphant's *Alphaville* (2020), which meshes blackened death metal with cascading drums, dissonant jazz and horns, co-produced by Mr Bungle's Trey Spruance and the ever-present Colin Marston. There's Barús, Supercontinent, Black Curse, Afterbirth – all of whom are creating wildly different sounds that have never been heard before, exploring a new realm beyond life as our understanding of death develops. And there are bands like Carcass, whose 2021 record *Torn Arteries* was rapturously received, clearly in their house style but made with wild passion, the joyful soundtrack to many of my late-night edit sessions.

Just as the universe is harder to map the further we get from the Big Bang, death metal's story is expanding rapidly, and all of these attitudes sit side by side in chaotic harmony. All of these are legitimate ways to stare into the face of death, and to welcome the crush of the end of the world together.

This chapter contains a mere surface scraping of death metal today. These practitioners are still working out their sounds and actively evolving, but all of them have some element that links back to the attitudes and values of the past: of scratching away at the dread and panic of being alive and projecting that horror into words and music. Death metal has diversified to an extreme degree, and all signs suggest it will continue to do so over the next decade.

7 Death wins

A man with a glassy stare looms over his subordinate. His colleagues bury themselves in work, the busy room bathing in the mid-morning sun. As he prepares a condemnation for missing another staff meeting, he is cut off by a stab of noise from overclocked speakers, signalling that the price of Bitcoin has dipped below a certain threshold. The office recoils.

We return to Napalm Death's 'You Suffer', which features in Season 5, Episode 3 of the HBO comedy series *Silicon Valley*.[1] Used here, the track is a subversion of the plastic, happy-go-lucky lifestyle promised by big tech.

The contrast is fun, a little Easter egg for death metal fanatics, and a reminder that death always wins. It permeates our lives, dominating our thoughts, our media, our politics and sometimes our music. For the same reason it's always there, patiently awaiting our inevitable demise, some representation of death has remained fascinating to musicians through time, and death metal has endured. Like death itself, the blast beats and harsh vocals persist, as mortals strain themselves to the point of exhaustion, if only to get a little more life in before they're snuffed out.

As this book is being written, death metal is approaching its fortieth birthday. Our fundamental approach to death and dying hasn't changed, but the culture and the environments that bands create in have. In this history, death metal has faced a great many challenges from both outside and within. While some of those challenges, such as overreaching government censorship, have gone too far, there are those of us who love this music dearly while finding some of its depictions, particularly of women, to be a potentially damaging distraction from the cut and thrust of death metal's core message.

Reckoning

Earlier, I wrote how I was uncomfortable with depictions of violent misogyny in death metal. I find it hard to enjoy a track like Cannibal Corpse's 'Fucked with a Knife', which speaks less of the universality of death and more of a hyper-focused, anti-women sentiment. Especially as a young adult it was difficult to immerse myself in subjects like this, and yet it seemed baked into the fabric of the genre. I wanted to know whether attitudes like this were totally locked in, or if they could be weeded out.

'I never thought I'd see the day honestly, but I have noticed a pretty profound shift in the past five years,' says Kim Kelly, who has a lifetime of writing about misogyny in extreme metal for *Terrorizer*, *MetalSucks* and *The Guardian*. 'Death metal bands who are coming out now have grown up on the older stuff, and it seems like the current generation is more conscious about these things, and maybe they aren't entirely straight cis dudes, so they have a little more perspective.'

Kelly continues,

> The trend of violent misogyny, rape fetishes, the glorification of violence against women – I think that's something that a lot of death metal fans today have actively tried to avoid, if not subvert. It doesn't take that much poetic creativity to write a song like 'Stripped, Raped, and Strangled', especially

if you grew up on horror movies and you're steeped in that whole aesthetic, which has always been the excuse, right? 'Oh it's just horror movie stuff.' Well, OK, do you have to watch those ones?

Researching this book whilst flitting between the rolling coverage of violence against women, which has been thankfully more out in the open since the Me Too movement began, made me profoundly uncomfortable. Violence is prevalent through all walks of human life, and death metal is refreshing for the way it explores it head on, but there is something distinctly dishonest about listening to early Cannibal Corpse or Prostitute Disfigurement, and brushing them off as unproblematic.

Recalling my earlier discussions with David Burke about why we make this music, I wonder: *Is death metal in this case discussing violence as a means of confronting the infinite? Or are we just exerting power over marginalised groups?*

As Kim Kelly outlined, there are movements within the scene that aim to fight against these voices, to kick back so these themes are no longer as prevalent. Then there are artists, like Venom Prison's Larissa Stupar, who are hitting back with rape-revenge fantasies on their own.

'English is not my first language, so when I was 12, 13, 14, I did not understand what they were singing about, and when I found out, and I could never let it go,' Stupar tells me.

> I did not feel like I should be listening to that kind of music because it's really misogynistic. So when we started Venom Prison, and we were writing [Venom Prison's 2016 album] *Animus*, I really wanted to have a song ['Perpetrator Emasculation'] where we kinda turned the tables on this and showed that women aren't just victims, we don't wanna

be victimised. As someone who is a rape survivor, I've really
wanted to bring my emotions to this situation.

The Cannibal Corpse saga is mixed, and there is no satisfactory answer. They continue to play the Chris Barnes-era tracks live, and outside the realm of their art, their long-time guitarist Pat O'Brien was arrested on assault and burglary charges in 2018.[2] However, attitudes have clearly changed for them; aside from Kelly's example, the uncensored art for 2021's well-received Violence Unimagined depicts a female figure surrounded by male corpses. It's perhaps a little jarring that the female form is still seen as something monstrous to the mind of death metal fans, but she is clearly the figure with agency here rather than the victim.

Violent misogyny doesn't do anything positive for death metal; it alienates potential fans and doesn't help anyone confront the rush of death. Real life violence towards women is not inevitable, and there are few who would miss its total expulsion. Unfortunately, these issues never happen in a vacuum, and often inform other unsavoury aspects.

Splitting the scene

Whilst misogyny flares up again and again in death metal art and lyrics, issues of race and sexuality are discussed less frequently. But people are clearly still making death metal from all over the world, and from all walks of life. Keith Kahn-Harris's early statement that it's impossible to make broad generalizations rings true here. Looking forward, I wanted to ask what is being done to make the scene better place?

'I'm noticing more young bands who are willing to speak out on [social] issues in a very positive and firm way,' says *Hell Bent for Metal's* Tom Dare,

> I think there are more people who have come up through
> the scene themselves and are helping those bands [with
> LGBT+ members] get up there, people who are willing to put
> on shows, run labels, start festivals, outlets like *Astral Noize*.
> It's really boring but what's going to really change things and
> stop these problems is just people being out. It's not bands,
> it's not labels, it's not flags – it's ordinary human contact.

'I think generally getting A&R people, marketing people,
and advertising people to think outside of the box, to think
more about diversity and the quality of the content, instead
of the aesthetics would help,' says *What Are You Doing Here?*
author Laina Dawes. 'They also need to do background checks
on the artists, regardless of whether a band is hot or they
know the singer. They've got to check to make sure they're
not involved in any nefarious groups, or it will come back to
haunt you.'

Dawes also believes that venues and promoters can also
make a huge difference in shaping the community in a positive
way.

'I wanna do a symposium to talk to people who own venues
about: *How do you set up for a show? Who are your security guys?
Who are your staff getting to make sure that there's diversity
training or whatever you wanna call it?*' she says.

> That's what needs to be done in terms of really making sure
> that this genre keeps on moving forward, because it could
> all just disintegrate. We need to get more young death metal
> bands to revitalise the scene, but you need to realise those
> young bands might not look like they did in the 1980s, and
> you have to accept that instead of saying, 'No, people aren't
> gonna want to see a Black singer.' They actually will, but you
> have to allow them that opportunity.

For anyone worried that the genre could lose its edge for the sake of inclusivity, Kim Kelly points out that death metal doesn't have to stop being outrageous:

> Even a band like Vastum, and the kinda psychosexual stuff they're exploring, is a much more interesting way to approach this stuff. It's still gross and weird and uncomfortable, but it's not actively oppressing anyone or making people feel like they don't belong. I think you can be gross and weird and violent without actively trying to negate someone's humanity – like, be an equal opportunities serial killer if you must.

The genre's uncomfortable introspection digs deep into the heart of what it means to make death metal, forcing it to consider real-life injustices as well as death in the abstract sense. Efforts to diversity the scene are increasingly welcome; death is for everyone, and singing about suffering from new perspectives, as Venom Prison have done, makes the scene richer. New voices speaking from new experiences allow for a deeper and more personal approach to what it means to fear and celebrate death.

Whether death metal will be used as protest music remains to be seen. The curious mix of extreme emotions, with the ferocious death growl, makes it excellent for communicating and exploring a shared horror like the fear of death, but less as a vehicle for expressing complex theory to outsiders. There is a reason that folk songs are sung and not growled. But it is heartening for those who have been immersed in the scene for a while to see a broader scope of participants.

'Your art is what you make of it and what you do with it,' says Kim Kelly.

Death metal doesn't get the mainstream respect or artistic regard that perhaps it deserves, but it still holds plenty of value and is incredibly important to a lot of people. When you're in a death metal band, people pay attention to what you say in interviews and on your records. If you want to use that platform you have to advance the cause of justice and liberation, then good for you.

Persistence

Death always wins, and death metal persists because there is some virtue in playing as hard as a human can play, snatching little moments of life from the jaws of the inevitable. The techniques persist because they represent the pinnacle of human ability – and when we bring machines in, they often replicate these sounds in the mission of pushing the same boundaries forward. And so the sound of death metal resists the jaws of time. Looking into the future, it will be a while before we can upload our consciousness into machines and live without the fear of death. Hopefully that means music like this will be around for some time to come.

In my many interviews for this book, everyone I spoke to was keen to talk about what death metal is doing today, excited to plug their friends or draw attention to something that was inspiring them. And everyone had a positive spin on where the genre is now and where it will go next.

'It's very easy to record songs and produce them yourself, to get a broad audience,' says Obscura's Steffen Kummerer. 'These days you have festivals like Wacken, Summer Breeze, With Full Force – they are as big as Oktoberfest. If you wear a Cradle of Filth shirt in the street it's normal, nobody cares anymore. The big question is, what will be the next thing to upset your neighbours?'

'I see a lot of young bands trying what we tried, to push the genre forward without losing the core of what it's supposed to be about,' Tomas Lindberg considers. 'Swedish bands like Morbus Chron and Rise From the Ashes, or Portal from Australia, are still finding new ways to make it interesting. That could be the future Morbid Angel or Autopsy; when we're in the retirement home that will be like The Beatles. It'll be interesting to see how that ages, if people still think it's just noise.'

Given how normalized the genre has become, there is a sense that this music isn't so shocking anymore. *Has death metal lost its bite? Are we used to it?* Certainly, when I revisit older records, the effect isn't the same as when I was thirteen. We are no longer the sweet babes who happened across *Tomb of the Mutilated*, and we need harder stuff.

But new generations bring with them new ways of experiencing music about being destroyed. Per Kim Kelly's recommendation, I found myself revolted and intrigued by Vastum's thoroughly horny marriage of sex, death and sordid gore. And the sprawling tales of clandestine alien intrusions from Blood Incantation were so singularly sinister that they genuinely haunted me.

During the Covid-19 pandemic, bands shifted away from older approaches of releasing records and made the jump to filming live or pre-recorded, audience-less performances. These were intended to be a fill-in for live shows, and, without the crush of an audience they sometimes looked a little static. But, to take Blood Incantation's performance at Adult Swim Festival, there was a magic to seeing a death metal band reduced to their component parts, and a strange energy to watching this alone in isolation. After all, we all die alone eventually.

Given death metal's morose tone, it's weird that my interviews were all thoroughly warm and uplifting, with well-spoken people who shared their optimistic hopes for the future. With shows and tours coming back, people told me tales of making up for lost time and celebrating the drive towards death with as many people as possible. Similarly, they were all excited about how the internet and technology are continuing death metal's evolution; the internet has made it so that anyone with even a passing interest can indulge themselves, even if just for an afternoon of exploration. And for anyone with the wherewithal to make this sort of music, the potential for it to be shared instantly – through Facebook groups, or in snippets in Instagram stories or on TikTok videos – is enormous.

'I feel like the future is like … everything!' says Colin Marston.

Think about how much music has changed in the last 20 years. Think about what music is gonna sound like in 1,000 years. If there are still humans, if we haven't blown ourselves up, what's metal gonna sound like? At that point maybe metal and reggaeton have merged, nursery rhymes and goregrind, anything you could think of. The only thing that's guaranteed is this continued evolution. So I don't agree with the idea that metal is gonna die. Music that was dead is being brought back because people are picking around the internet every second of every day, finding this form of folk music from this country from a thousand years ago, incorporating that into metal, and giving that a new life. Pure chaos – that's your answer.

Future deaths

It's 2021, and I am at England's Bloodstock Open Air festival, having not showered for four days. I am watching Beyond Extinction, five teenagers from Essex who won a regional competition to play a stage for newcomers. The afternoon sun is savage and the ground outside is scorched, trampled bare by marauding metalheads dressed as vikings. The frontman, too young to grow a beard, cries out for war crimes to be committed in the circle pit, which immediately opens. The respect the crowd have for him is immense, and they get to work.

Later on, Judas Priest headline a much larger stage. Performing 'Halls of Valhalla', frontman Rob Halford switches from his trademark high-pitched wail to an unearthly death growl, a genuinely unexpected change in register that sends ripples of excitement through the crowd.

I am at the end of editing this book, living through the second year of the pandemic, taking a break to do what I would generously call field research. I feel a lot of things: physically exhausted, lightly perturbed by the war crimes request, a little worried I might get kicked in the face. But after not seeing any live music for nearly eighteen months, watching bona fide death metal bands spew their guts up on stage is a near religious experience.

Death contains a lot of things, and so does death metal. It can be melodic and triumphant like Fleshgod Apocalypse, or on the cusp of disintegrating into noise, like Portal. As fond as I am, I find some of it tasteless and revolting, and have written about those examples with strong content warnings. Some of it I discussed with people in whispered breaths, both of us feeling a little uneasy. Where it's listed here, it comes with the caveat that it's a poor representation of a genre that I personally love and want more people to enjoy. In eighteen months of death and turmoil, knowing there was a genre of music that explored these ugly parts of human existence was a conscious reminder that death unites us.

Through this book, the focus has been on telling an emotional history of death metal, which naturally makes it a little personal. Through my life, death metal in some form has been a constant. I've met close friends and formed relationships around a shared passion and leaned on it when times were rough. Through it, I've come to terms with my own eventual death and the deaths of my loved ones. There's magic in the waves of drama, where every hammer blow is another short step closer to the final crush of nothingness. And though many books could be spent picking apart the threads of emotion, it's comforting to know that something of the appeal of death metal is, ultimately, ineffable.

'It's got to say something that, after all these years, and all the things I've been through and witnessed and interrogated and reported on, death metal is still my comfort food,' Kim Kelly reflects. 'It sticks with you. It sticks to your ribs.'

10 Essential tracks

1. Possessed – Death Metal – 1985

Thrash metal's dark undercurrent had been looking for a new voice, and found it in Jeff Beracca. Nothing sounded like this before, where the harsher vocals were married with gruffer riffs and extreme speed. His new technique finally matched the horrific lyrics about being tormented by armies of the dead, who rule over the hapless living as the sun slowly fades to black. Crucially, this is written from the perspective of the dead themselves; this is death in a moment of triumph.

2. Napalm Death – You Suffer – 1987

Sometimes death is a mercilessly slow process. Sometimes it's a gradual but steady decline, allowing a few moments to reflect before the void consumes. And sometimes the whole process starts and concludes before the human brain has time to respond. 'You Suffer' is such a song. With no equal in brevity, it's the absolute end point of songwriting economy, posing a question and refusing time for contemplation. The reaction is elicits most is humour, a perfectly valid answer to an unanswerable question and a sensible reaction to the crush of infinity.

3. Carcass – Manifestation of Verrucose Urethra – 1998

The first effect of death is the slow decay of the body, the invasion of bacteria and insects as the human form decomposes into nutrients. Vital though this is, it's a disgusting process. Here, this is magnified a hundred times. We can all imagine what a cadaver looks like, but learning medical terms in exact detail gives the scene a repulsive clarity, even if some of those concepts are themselves a little mangled. Compared to the existential perils of some other bands, the early Carcass efforts are decidedly human.

4. Cannibal Corpse – Hammer Smashed Face – 1992

At stop signs, in line at the bank, in tedious meetings, violence festers inside us. Over years it grows before it's suddenly released. Celebrating this urge, Cannibal Corpse flash a brief, complex bass fill – the last moment of cognition – before the red mist takes over. Bassist Alex Webster's heavy groove anchors this song from flying in too many directions; this is simply about being overcome by bloodlust, acting on impulse in a splatter of viscera as repressed the emotions rush over you.

5. At the Gates – Slaughter of the Soul – 1995

Death metal thrives on dissonance. The warp of the voice from soaring and graceful to the baleful roar of the death growl is one of the cornerstones of the genre, so the instruments might be expected to follow suit. 'Slaughter of the Soul' is the sweet taste of almond in the cyanide, a little sting of something pleasant that makes what follows all the more powerful. The song itself concerns disillusionment and could be read as a murder or suicide narrative, the forbidden dopamine release of knife cutting into flesh.

6. Death – Spirit Crusher – 1998

The slow stripping of the soul is among the more dehumanizing forms of death. Whether this comes from internal self-criticism or external negative feedback, the draining of energy is one of the most harrowing forms of slowly dying, especially mortifying for creative types hampered by internal and external factors, as Death experienced through their career. In a similar way to the buildup of rage in 'Hammer Smashed Face', the anguish this time is directed inwards, with the narrator struggling between succumbing to the darkness and holding on. Reflecting this, the instrumentation flits between a rush of notes and simple rhythms, building and releasing tension, enduring and then releasing emotion.

7. Opeth – The Leper Affinity – 2001

A dimly-lit tale of a strained relationship, Opeth lean into a detailed, gloomy narrative. Abuse, banishment and relationship trauma are framed against the backdrop of the freezing winter. A far cry from Cannibal Corpse, they diversify their sound in order to tackle more nuanced topics, with the decay of a relationship framed as parallel to human death. Opeth contrast death metal's iron fist with a lace glove, providing more energy when the weighty guitars come back with more power.

8. Job for a Cowboy – Entombment of a Machine – 2007

Death metal emerged into the digital era with the rise of deathcore, and fittingly this is about the torture and imprisonment of a machine. Job for a Cowboy play a busy version of the style, cascading through riffs and rhythms and switching up the vocal style by introducing a new dynamic, a clean voice that contrasts the growl. The technicality of older bands is reimagined into something with more rhythmic variance, benefiting from a generation of production engineers building on their skills. Proof that youthful, wiry music could be made about oblivion by younger people who were very distant from their own deaths.

9. Venom Prison – Perpetrator Emasculation – 2016

Violent misogyny festers in the dark hearts of death metal's history. Venom Prison takes charge of the situation, re-framing the situation as the gruesome castration of a rapist. Awful to behold, death, punishment and torture are re-considered through a lens that's critical of the male gaze. For older fans, this is difficult to reckon with, an uncomfortable challenge that's been left to fester for too long. Questions may persist over whether gendered violence has a place at all, but there's a subversive power to kicking back against lazy, ugly attitudes and an undeniable dark power to the track.

10. Cryptic Shift – Moonbelt Immolator – 2020

Labyrinthine, psychedelic, Byzantine, 'Moonbelt Immolator' is a free and expressive version of death metal. Bafflingly complex, the track is dense with new ideas that spiral out into wild new worlds, clashing tales of interstellar conflicts, astral cryptids and abandoned mining operations, set against the backdrop of space. The blastbeats and death growls are all still here, but stretched and warped to a 20+ minute runtime, taking a good stab at listing all the myriad ways you can meet an ignominious end in space.

At a time when we're gazing out to the stars, it's a reminder that the deaths that wait beyond the furthest reaches of humanity are likely to be the darkest yet.

Notes

Chapter 1

1 'Ed Miliband Learns to Sing Extreme Metal'. N.d. *BBC News*. Accessed 6 March 2021. https://www.bbc.co.uk/news/av/uk–40358874.

2 'You Suffer (Miliband Edition)'. N.d. www.youtube.com. Accessed 7 March 2021. https://www.youtube.com/watch?v=0fi8UjeXIj0&ab_channel=EaracheRecords.

3 'Napalm Death Streams Have Soared Thanks to Ed Miliband'. 2017. *NME*. https://www.nme.com/news/music/napalm-death-streams-have-soared-thanks-to-ed-miliband–2092159.

4 'Blood Incantation: Hidden History of the Human Race'. 2019. *Pitchfork.Com*. https://pitchfork.com/reviews/albums/blood-incantation-hidden-history-of-the-human-race/.

5 'Coldplay: A Rush of Blood to the Head'. *Pitchfork*. 2002 https://pitchfork.com/reviews/albums/1538-a-rush-of-blood-to-the-head/.

6 'U2: How to Dismantle an Atomic Bomb'. 2004. *Pitchfork*. https://pitchfork.com/reviews/albums/8330-how-to-dismantle-an-atomic-bomb/.

Chapter 2

1 Phull, Hardeep. 2012. 'Protest Songs: Marching to the Beat of Dissent'. *The Independent*. https://www.independent.co.uk/

arts-entertainment/music/features/protest-songs-marching-
to-the-beat-of-dissent-7619263.html.

2 Doran, John. 2010. 'The Quietus | Features | A Quietus
    Interview | Forging Black Metal: Cronos of Venom Talks about
    the Genesis of a Genre'. *The Quietus*. https://thequietus.com/
    articles/03544-forging-black-metal-cronos-of-venom-talks-
    about-the-genesis-of-a-genre.

3 'Various – Metal Massacre VI'. 2021. *Discogs*. Accessed
    February 28. https://www.discogs.com/release/1793379-
    Various-Metal-Massacre-VI.

4 Dom Lawson, 'Interview with Mick Harris'. Liner notes for
    Grind Madness at the BBC: The Earache Peel Sessions, 2009,
    CD, 4.

5 Mudrian, Albert. 2004. *Choosing Death*. Los Angeles, CA: Feral
    House, 125.

6 Mudrian, Albert. 2004. *Choosing Death*. Los Angeles, CA: Feral
    House, 133–4.

Chapter 3

1 Mudrian, Albert. 2004. *Choosing Death*. Los Angeles, CA: Feral
    House, 162.

2 Mudrian, Albert. 2004. *Choosing Death*. Los Angeles, CA: Feral
    House, 91.

3 Mudrian, Albert. 2004. *Choosing Death*. Los Angeles, CA: Feral
    House, 164.

4 Mudrian, Albert. 2004. *Choosing Death*. Los Angeles, CA: Feral
    House, 125. https://web.archive.org/web/20100430153146/

http://blogcritics.org/music/article/cannibal-corpse-is-top-selling-death

5   'Best-Selling Album'. 2021. *Guinness World Records*. Accessed January 30. https://www.guinnessworldrecords.com/world-records/70133-best-selling-album.

6   Mudrian, Albert. 2004. *Choosing Death*. Los Angeles, CA: Feral House, 181.

7   'Films And Recordings Threaten Nation's Character, Dole Says (Published 1995)'. 1995. *Nytimes.Com*. https://www.nytimes.com/1995/06/01/us/films-and-recordings-threaten-nation-s-character-dole-says.html.

8   'Read an Exclusive Excerpt from "Relentless: 30 Years of Sepultura"'. 2014. *Vice.Com*. https://www.vice.com/en/article/68wzxr/exclusive-excerpt-relentless.

Chapter 4

1   'Nå Slipper «Greven» Ut | TV 2 Nyhetene'. *Web.Archive.Org*. https://web.archive.org/web/20090312025704/http://www.tv2nyhetene.no/innenriks/krim/article2614786.ece.

2   Mudrian, Albert. 2004. *Choosing Death*. Los Angeles, CA: Feral House, 187.

3   Mudrian, Albert. 2004. *Choosing Death*. Los Angeles, CA: Feral House, 188.

4   'Carcass'. 2022. *Goddamnbastard.Org*. Accessed 30 January. http://www.goddamnbastard.org/carcass/interviews/rockhard111.html.

Chapter 5

1   'Rock Hard Vol. 104'. 2021. *ROCK HARD Heavy-Metal-Magazine*.
    Accessed April 30. https://www.rockhard.de/megazine/
    heft_43753.html.

2   'The 100 Greatest Metal Albums of All Time'. 2017. *Rolling
    Stone*. http://www.rollingstone.com/music/music-lists/the-
    100-greatest-metal-albums-of-all-time–113614/.

3   'KNOTFEST Roadshow'. 2022. *KNOTFEST Roadshow*. Accessed
    31 July. https://web.archive.org/web/20190306044713/
    https://www.knotfestroadshow.com/.

4   Rosenberg, Axl and Vince Neilstein. 2007. 'CINEMETAL: SUICIDE
    SILENCE, "THE PRICE OF BEAUTY" | Metalsucks'. *Metalsucks*.
    https://www.metalsucks.net/2007/10/30/cinemetal-suicide-
    silence-the-price-of-beauty/.

5   'BLABBERMOUTH.NET – JOB FOR A COWBOY's "Ruination"
    Lands on BILLBOARD Chart'. 2009. *Web.Archive.Org*. https://
    web.archive.org/web/20090718112157/http://www.
    roadrunnerrecords.com/blabbermouth.net/news.aspx?mode
    =Article&newsitemID=123627.

6   'JOB FOR A COWBOY: "Demonocracy" First-Week Sales
    Revealed'. 2012. *BLABBERMOUTH.NET*. https://www.
    blabbermouth.net/news/job-for-a-cowboy-demonocracy-
    first-week-sales-revealed/.

Chapter 6

1   'Lil Mariko & Full Tac, the Couple behind Cursed Anthem
    Where's My Juul?'. 2020. *I-D*. https://i-d.vice.com/

en_uk/article/m7qg73/wheres-my-juul-full-tac-lil-mariko-interview.

2 'A Beginner's Guide to Dissonant Death Metal'.
   2021. *Bandcamp Daily*. https://daily.bandcamp.com/lists/
   dissonant-death-metal-list.

3 'The Twisted Sounds of German Technical Death Metal'.
   2018. *Bandcamp Daily*. https://daily.bandcamp.com/scene-
   report/german-tech-death-metal-list.

4 'Huge Sharks Love Death Metal, Film Crew Finds Out'.
   2015. *The Independent*. https://www.independent.
   co.uk/news/science/death-metal-music-attracts-sharks-
   documentary-crew-finds-out-10381295.html.

5 'Doom Eternal Shows Off Its Heavy Metal Choir'.
   2020. *Pcgamer*. https://www.pcgamer.com/uk/doom-
   eternal-shows-off-its-heavy-metal-choir/.

6 'Brütal Legend Soundtrack'. 2020. *Brütal Legend Wiki*. https://
   brutallegend.fandom.com/wiki/Soundtrack.

7 'Setlist in Guitar Hero: Warriors of Rock'. 2021. *Wikihero*.
   Accessed 17 September. https://guitarhero.fandom.com/
   wiki/Setlist_in_Guitar_Hero:_Warriors_of_Rock.

8 'Cross-Dressing, J Pop and Death Metal: A Day in the Life of
   Aussie Wrestler Ladybeard'. 2016. *Vice.Com*. https://www.
   vice.com/en/article/ezeyee/cross-dressing-j-pop-and-death-
   metal-a-day-in-the-life-of-aussie-wrestler-ladybeard.

9 @Justin_SofOK. Twitter Post. 26 June 2021, 11:05 PM. https://
   twitter.com/i/status/1408909400341979140.

10 'Juric'S Death Metal Approach Has Made Torino a Devilish
   Team to Face | Nicky Bandini'. 2022. *The Guardian*. https://
   www.theguardian.com/football/2022/jan/17/ivan-juric-
   death-metal-approach-torino-devilish-team-serie-a.

11 Grierson, Jamie. "Virginia Elects Transgender Woman to State Legislature." The Guardian, Guardian News and Media, 8 Nov. 2017, https://www.theguardian.com/us-news/2017/nov/08/danica-roem-virginia-first-transgender-person-elected-state-legislature.

12 'This Is the Most Expensive Death Metal Logo Hoodie Ever!'. 2016. Metalinjection.Net. https://metalinjection.net/fashion/this-is-the-most-expensive-death-metal-logo-hoodie-ever.

Chapter 7

1 Neilstein, Vince and Axl Rosenberg. 2018. 'Napalm Death's "You Suffer" Featured Prominently in New Episode of HBO's Silicon Valley | Metalsucks'. *Metalsucks*. https://www.metalsucks.net/2018/04/09/napalm-deaths-you-suffer-featured-prominently-in-new-episode-of-hbos-silicon-valley/.

2 'Former Cannibal Corpse Guitarist Pat O'brien Sentenced for Role in Bizarre Burglary'. 2021. *NME*. https://www.nme.com/news/music/former-cannibal-corpse-guitarist-pat-obrien-sentenced-for-role-in-bizarre-burglary–2933009.

Selected bibliography

BANGERTV – All Metal. 2015. 'Metal Evolution – Extreme Metal | FULL EPISODE'. *YouTube*. https://www.youtube.com/watch?v=MoHOgfEoTlc.

Belalcazar, Felipe, dir. N.d. *Death by Metal*.

Berger, Harris M. 1999. *Metal, Rock, and Jazz : Perception and the Phenomenology of Musical Experience*. Hanover, NH: University Press of New England.

'Carcass – the Pathologist's Report Part 1: Incubation (Official Documentary)'. N.d. www.youtube.com. Accessed 7 December 2021. https://www.youtube.com/watch?v=-enFT6j08vA.

'Carcass – the Pathologist's Report Part 2: Propagation (Official Documentary)'. N.d. www.youtube.com. Accessed 7 December 2021. https://www.youtube.com/watch?v=r67Hte5cgvU.

'Carcass – the Pathologist's Report Part 3: Mass Infection (Official Documentary)'. N.d. www.youtube.com. Accessed 7 December 2021. https://www.youtube.com/watch?v=3LztlhMpaos.

'Carcass – the Pathologist's Report Part 4: Epidemic (Official Documentary)'. N.d. www.youtube.com. Accessed 7 December 2021. https://www.youtube.com/watch?v=3hjqCYX5bvk.

'Carcass – the Pathologist's Report Part 5: Decomposition (Official Documentary)'. N.d. www.youtube.com. Accessed 7 December 2021. https://www.youtube.com/watch?v=nWFUUqujDdQ.

Dunn, Sam, dir. 2008. *Global Metal*. Streamed: Seville Pictures, Warner Home Video.

Ekeroth, Daniel. 2008. *Swedish Death Metal*. Brooklyn, NY: Bazillion Points Books.

Glasper, Ian. 2009. *Trapped in a Scene : UK Hardcore 1985–89*. London: Cherry Red Books.

Glasper, Ian. 2014. *Burning Britain : The History of UK Punk 1980–1984*. Oakland, CA: Pm Press.

Hardeep, Phull. 2012. 'Protest Songs: Marching to the Beat of Dissent'. *The Independent*, 4 April 2012. https://www.independent.co.uk/arts-entertainment/music/features/protest-songs-marching-to-the-beat-of-dissent-7619263.html.

Hegarty, Paul. 2013. *Noise/Music a History*. New York, London, Oxford, New Delhi and Sydney: Bloomsbury Academic: An Imprint of Bloomsbury Publishing Inc.

Kahn-Harris, Keith. 2007. *Extreme Metal : Music and Culture on the Edge*. Oxford and New York: Berg.

'KNOTFEST Roadshow'. 2019. *Web.archive.org*. 6 March 2019. https://web.archive.org/web/20190306044713/https://www.knotfestroadshow.com/.

Laina, Dawes. 2012. *What Are You Doing Here?: A Black Woman's Life and Liberation in Heavy Metal*. Brooklyn, NY: Bazillion Points.

Mudrian, Albert. 2016. *Choosing Death : The Improbable History of Death Metal & Grindcore*. New York City, United States: Bazillion Points.

'Napalm Death – the Scum Story [Official Full Documentary]'. N.d. www.youtube.com. Accessed 7 December 2021. https://www.youtube.com/watch?v=7rixjwzl6P4.